YEAR-ROUND
LOW-FAT
HOLIDAY
MEALS
in Minutes!

**MORE THAN
200 DELICIOUS
AND HEALTHY
RECIPES FOR OVER
20 HOLIDAYS AND
SPECIAL EVENTS**

by M.J. Smith, R.D.

CHRONIMED PUBLISHING

Year-Round Low-Fat Holiday Meals in Minutes! More than 200 Delicious and Healthy Recipes for Over 20 Holidays and Special Events ©1995 by M.J. Smith, R.D.

ISBN 1-56561-074-1

Edited by: Jolene Steffer
Cover Design: Terry Dugan Design
Text Design: Liana Vaiciulis Raudys
Art/Production Manager: Claire Lewis
Production Artist: Janet Hogge
Printed in the United States of America

Published by
Chronimed Publishing
P.O. Box 59032
Minneapolis, MN 55459-9686

DEDICATION

This book is dedicated to all the people who have deepened my appreciation for holidays.

◆ *The people I still call "Daddy and Mother," who came from small families (I have no first cousins), but continue to make every holiday a big deal.*

◆ *To a group of people known as "the Brase clan," who knew how to eat and laugh in a big way, and adopted our family for many holidays.*

◆ *To the family I have grown to know and love in my married life—the Parsons/Smith gang and their leader, Martha Isabelle Parsons Smith.*

ACKNOWLEDGMENTS

This book was written with the best holiday ideas from my network of friends. Their names are mentioned with the recipes and they know I am grateful.

Thank you to Kate Merrick, who took time away from her family during her first college Christmas break to assist with nutrient analysis.

And to a new-found professional associate who has edited and reworked much of this manuscript, Michele Gaffney-Rabik. I thank God you landed in my corner of the world.

ABOUT THE AUTHOR

M.J. Smith is a registered dietitian and cookbook author. Her previous books include *All American Low-Fat Meals in Minutes; 60 Days of Low-Cost, Low-Fat Meals in Minutes; 366 Low-Fat Recipes in Minutes;* and *The Miracle Foods Cookbook.*

Ms. Smith lives with her husband and two children in Guttenberg, Iowa. Her writing office is located on the banks of the Mississippi River. She regularly contributes nutrition commentary to national magazines, including *Good Taste* and *Diabetes in the News.* Aside from writing, she continues her dietetic practice at the Guttenberg Municipal Hospital.

The inspiration for this book was her personal experience of trying to marry traditional celebration foods with her low-fat lifestyle.

NOTICE:
CONSULT HEALTH CARE PROFESSIONAL

Readers are advised to seek the guidance of a licensed physician or health care professional before making any changes in prescribed health care regimens, as each individual case or need may vary. This book is intended for informational purposes only and is not for use as an alternative to appropriate medical care. While every effort has been made to ensure that the information is the most current available, new research findings, being released with increased frequency, may invalidate some data.

CONTENTS

Menu Ideas and Over 200 Recipes for

VIII

INTRODUCTION

What's the secret to a happy holiday? The food! Of course, it's not quite that simple. But holiday eating experiences often transcend the most beautiful decorations and expensive gifts to make lasting memories.

When I became an adult and started taking my turn hosting holiday gatherings, I found myself irritable and tired by the time we sat down to the main meal. And I still had to clean-up and put whiney children to bed. Time and experience have mellowed my holiday style. I haven't thrown out the lemon pie at Easter or the Christmas cranberries, but I have changed my focus.

This book is a blend of classic holiday recipes with the simple low-fat and no-fat entertaining style of the '90s. Inside, you'll find 31 fat-free recipes, 21 with only 1 gram of fat per serving, and 61 recipes with 2 or 3 grams of fat per serving. *Year-Round Low-Fat Holiday Meals in Minutes!* has been written to help you enjoy creating food experiences for your family and friends in the context of good health. You're probably wondering how that can be possible and delicious at the same time.

The first 30 or so pages of this book provide a guide to getting organized with a realistic budget of time and money. The holiday sections that follow have simple symbols and tips for keeping the traditional feel and message to the celebration.

And now to the food. As mentioned earlier, this is a collection of lower-fat and no-fat versions of traditional holiday menus and recipes. The calories have been reduced, but the taste retained.

You will look at a few of the recipes and say, "Well, there's more than 25% fat in this." And you're right, but would your brother-in-law swallow pumpkin pie without a crust or quiche topped with fake cheese?

Notice the portions of fruits, vegetables, and grains are large because it's better to have seconds of the vegetable casserole than the pork loin. And you'll see mini-dessert portions, because six bites of a rich, creamy texture and delicious flavor go a long way.

And let's face it . . . many of us and our relatives struggle with weight, cholesterol, and diabetes control. Serving up healthy choices on the buffet table is an investment in many more holiday gatherings with everyone around the table!

A word about nutrient analysis:

◆ *If a brand-name food is mentioned, I have used that product in the recipe test.*

◆ *Cholesterol values using liquid egg substitutes are always noted.*

◆ *If you are using a food exchange plan for weight control or diabetes, look to the end of each analysis. These food group values are based on the Exchange List for Meal Planning, a system developed and published by the American Dietetic Association and the American Diabetes Association. Exchange values for recipes using a combination of fruits, vegetables, or grains are based on the food exchange group that most closely matches the final nutrient profile.*

◆ *Nutrient analysis of whole recipes into single portions is based on the rounding of carbohydrate, protein, and fat grams into whole numbers. This occasionally leads to minor discrepancies of up to 15 calories per serving. Recipes with less than 0.5 grams of fat or saturated fat per serving are rounded to 0 grams.*

◆ *The term "reduced-fat" refers to products with 50% less fat. Nonfat or fat-free products contain less than 1 gram of fat per serving. Recipes were tested with the specific type of ingredient listed.*

As you bite into this book and your own design for the perfect holiday, reflect on the following:

"A person is rich in proportion to the number of things which he can afford to let alone."—Thoreau

"There is only one success—to be able to spend your life in your own way."—Christopher Morley

"There is more to life than increasing its speed."—Gandhi

"I stopped believing in Santa Claus when my mother took me to see him in a department store, and he asked for my autograph."—Shirley Temple

"Life is short. Live it up."—Nikita Khrushchev

Holidays Without Weight Gain or Weariness

*O*ne need not be puritanical and count every fat gram in the holiday meal, but a little good sense will limit guilt and indigestion when the party is over. These strategies work for me:

If it's your turn to have Thanksgiving and the whole idea tenses you up, plan to "unstress." Take a warm bath; scrub yourself with one of those long-handled bath brushes. Limit caffeine and sugar. They may improve your mood and energy level for a short time, but they lead to fatigue later in the day. Consider rewarding yourself with a massage the week of the holiday preparations. Listen to uplifting music; it may be the Beatles, Mary Chapin Carpenter, or Vivaldi who produces joy for you. Buy an envelope or two of those room scents to freshen your environment and your mood.

Scientists are finding when you crave a certain food, your brain may be sending you a message. Carbohydrates boost serotonin in the brain, which produces a calming effect. Eat a toasted bagel or raisin English muffin with a spread of all-fruit jam, and allow at least an hour for the food to work. At meal time, include a lean protein source to get a dose of the amino acid tyrosine. Tyrosine combats the drowsiness associated with a high-carbohydrate meal.

As thoughts turn to a memorable menu for the holiday, plan high-bulk, low-fat appetizers that won't spoil dinner. Fresh vegetables (go ahead and splurge on tender asparagus spears) dipped in a reduced-fat salad dressing are always a winner. Or lightly stuff some celery with reduced-fat cheddar cheese spread and sprinkle with Italian or Mexican seasonings. Bread sticks, pretzels, and toasted pita bread triangles add crunch, but not fat, when you need something to go along with a welcoming cold drink.

If you tend to do too much tasting while you're cooking, keep your mouth busy with something else! Chew gum, suck on a sugarless breath mint, sip on herb tea or mineral water, or just go ahead and brush your teeth! Or sing along to some music instead of chewing!

When Aunt Mary calls and offers to bring that high fat rum cake as the traditional dessert, politely accept her offer. Then plan to offer a lower-fat alternative such as lemon sherbet with fresh fruit topping. The '90s has brought "fat awareness" to the forefront of many family conversations about food. One need not apologize for offering a healthy alternative at the reunion. When confronted by relatives who use holidays as an excuse to overindulge in fat, just look them in the eye when you take only a sliver of that rum cake and say, "I really enjoy a taste of your delicious cake." Or you can get right to the point and explain, "I will just feel better tomorrow if I limit my fat intake today." No one can argue with your honest feelings, and you are not pushing your food "values" onto anyone else.

If holiday celebrations last for several days, plan most of the menus to be lean and healthy. Refuse to dress up salads and vegetables with rich, creamy sauces and dressings. String beans with fresh chopped chives or a green salad with reduced-fat dressing will be enjoyed for their true flavors.

Get up and move around after that delicious dinner. I have included a whole section on games and activities that get you out and away from picking at the leftovers.

And finally, stay healthy after the holiday by following these tips to prevent the spread of colds and flu among family members:

◆ *Wash your hands often and have the children do the same.*

◆ *Use disposable tissues instead of handkerchiefs.*

◆ *Use disposable cups in the bathroom and kitchen, instead of sharing glasses.*

◆ *Wipe down "high touch" surfaces such as doorknobs and telephones frequently.*

◆ *Use antibacterial liquid soap; bacteria and viruses can linger on bar soap.*

◆ *Avoid smoking in the home. Smoke is a respiratory irritant that increases risk for colds and flu.*

◆ *Wash children's toys often in warm, soapy water.*

◆ *Clean kitchen utensils and counters with warm soapy water and let them air dry. Dish towels can be a haven for bacteria and viruses.*

◆ *Ventilate rooms frequently, as bacteria remain in stagnant air.*

Do It Ahead!

Every holiday will be more fun when you feel in control and organized. I don't mean keeping a minute-by-minute schedule of tasks . . . but rather a flexible plan that keeps you on track and yet allows you to enjoy the present moment.

It seems most of us have a passion for getting organized. Prepare for the holiday by removing extra clutter from your main living areas—the kitchen, the eating area, and the family room. Remove those things that you haven't used or appreciated in the last three months. Do you really need the bread baker, espresso machine, and toaster on your countertop? Do you really need 17 refrigerator magnets? You'll be surprised at how fresh and clean the room feels after all that clutter has been removed.

After clutter removal, you are free to sit down at the kitchen table or the breakfast bar and make a list (oh no. . . I said the "l" word). I use one or two half-sheets of paper for everything. If you get more than one or two lists going, you'll get lost among the lists. A sample follows after this section.

Manageable Menus and No-Hassle Shopping

The qualities of a winning holiday menu are:

—a dish that's old

—a recipe that's new

—and plenty of food from other people, too!

As you ponder "what in the world to fix," think about how you can serve the foods you already have on hand. For example:

◆ *You picked up frozen vegetables on special, so plan to steam them in the microwave. Or steam them, add chopped fresh onion and pepper, chill them, dress them up in reduced-fat ranch dressing, and you'll have a salad.*

◆ *You have a couple of loaves of frozen bread dough on hand. Plan to thaw them the night before the party and bake them as your guests arrive.*

◆ *Your pantry is full of canned beans: kidney beans, butter beans, and pork 'n' beans. Drain and then dump them into the crockpot, season with barbecue sauce or salsa, and plug it in first thing in the morning.*

◆ *Remember the ham or turkey your company gave you for Christmas? Plan that as the center of the meal and go from there.*

Next, what are you hungry for? If it's shrimp on the grill, that's fine. After all, this party is for you too. Then look over my menu ideas and select a couple of recipes that sound like fun to make. It's a bit unrealistic to try six or eight new things.

Go ahead and delegate everything else. Most people expect and want to bring something to share at holiday time. Suggestions for easy fill-ins might include:

◆ *a cold vegetable salad*

◆ *a fresh fruit plate for an appetizer*

◆ *a dessert the kids will enjoy*

◆ *a tasty bread to go with the grilled turkey*

◆ *a vegetable ready to microwave*

If all your bases haven't been covered with these steps, then go ahead and splurge at the deli counter. Fill out your menu with a clear-dressing coleslaw or pasta salad, a relish tray, or fresh onion rolls from the bakery.

Read over the new recipes you'll be trying, and make sure you have all the ingredients on hand. If you don't, be sure to add them to your grocery list.

Beverage Selection

Offering three beverage selections is plenty! There is no need to inventory six different kinds of soft drinks to suit everyone's palate.

Choose one from each of these lists:

SUGAR-FREE/CALORIE-FREE COLD DRINKS:

Mineral water
Diet soft drinks
Iced tea
Sugar-free lemonade
Sugar-free fruit drinks such as Koolaid®

NUTRITIOUS BEVERAGE CHOICES:

Skim or 1% milk
Low-fat chocolate milk
100% fruit juices such as orange-pineapple
Tomato juice or vegetable juice cocktail
Fruit juice/mineral water blends
Sparkling non-alcoholic fruit juice

FOR THE THIRD, GO AHEAD AND ADD A POPULAR SOFT DRINK.

Buy it in two-liter bottles to save money.

OPTION FOUR: CONSIDER A HOT BEVERAGE FOR DESSERT TIME:

Coffee or decaf
Flavored coffee
Espresso or cappuccino
Brewed tea
Herbal tea
Hot cider or apple juice

If you offer beer, wine, or mixed drinks at holiday time, consider these Responsible Party Tips from Anheuser-Busch:

◆ *Be sure everyone knows that overdrinking is unacceptable.*

◆ *Always serve food with alcoholic beverages; protein-containing foods moderate the effects of alcohol.*

◆ *Keep guests entertained with good food, activities, conversation, and a relaxed setting.*

◆ *Never force drinks on your guests. Resist the impulse to refill glasses the minute they are empty.*

◆ *When serving a mixed drink, always measure the liquor carefully.*

◆ *Set a good example and make your first drink nonalcoholic or low-alcohol. Drink slowly and try to limit your total intake to no more than two drinks.*

◆ *If someone has gone over the limit, simply put all of the alcohol away. Make sure everyone has a safe ride home with a designated driver.*

When selecting wine, drink what you like. If you want help, consult Barbara Ensrud's books, *Wine With Food* and *Best Wine Buys for $10 or Less*.

WHAT ABOUT SPARKLING DRINKS?

Many of us enjoy a glass of sparkling grape juice or champagne before a holiday meal. Remember that dry in champagne means not sweet. On labels commonly found in U.S. stores, "brut" is the driest, usually containing less than one percent sugar. Next comes "extra dry," which is still dry but fairly fruity. "Dry" is the sweetest of the three.

Serve sparkling drinks in a tall, narrow flute to make the most of the bubbles. Chill champagne well before serving.

To open a champagne bottle safely, pick up the bottle with your left hand, placing your thumb over the cork and pointing the top away from yourself and other people. Hold the bottle at a 45-degree angle and undo the wire with your right hand, keeping your thumb in place in case the cork pops off prematurely. Then hold the cork firmly in your left hand and the bottle in your right, and gently twist the two in opposite directions to allow the pressure in the bottle to be released slowly. Gently pull the two apart as you twist. The bottle should go "poof," not "pop." Always have a towel on hand, in case of a spillover, although this is unlikely unless the bottle has been shaken or is too warm. If the cork is stubborn, use the towel to grasp and turn it.

How to Set Up a Buffet Table

Buffet service is a practical way to serve large groups of holiday guests. Be sure the menu includes dishes that will hold their temperatures and textures well. On a buffet line, individual servings of foods add the look and feel of a sit-down meal. For instance, you may want to put hamburgers into buns and arrange them on a tray or put the fruit into individual cups. Avoid soups and other foods that spill easily. Consider pouring the beverages for your guests after they have seated themselves.

Try to include a few candles or a fruit bowl as a centerpiece, even if the buffet line is your kitchen counter.

When arranging foods on a buffet, use this logical scheme:

—Plates first

—Entree

—Starch or Potato

—Hot Vegetables

—Salad Items

—Bread

Wrap silverware in napkins and lay them out on a tray or place the sets of silverware at the table place settings.

If you don't serve beverages to your guests, consider having a separate area for beverages. This method will suggest to guests that they take their plates to the table first, and then serve themselves a beverage.

We Just Ran Out Of . . .
Common Ingredient Substitutions

Are you missing an ingredient? Here's a list to save the day.

RECIPE CALLS FOR:	TRY THIS INSTEAD:
1 CLOVE MINCED GARLIC	1/4 tsp. instant minced garlic or 1/8 tsp. garlic powder
1/2 CUP CHOPPED ONION	1 Tbsp. instant minced onion or 1 tsp. onion powder
1 TBSP. FRESH HERBS	1 tsp. dried herbs
1 CUP CHILI SAUCE	1 cup tomato sauce + 1/3 cup sugar + 2 Tbsp. vinegar
1 LB. FRESH MUSHROOMS	6 oz. canned mushrooms
1 TBSP. CORNSTARCH	2 Tbsp. flour

RECIPE CALLS FOR:	TRY THIS INSTEAD:
1 CUP PLAIN YOGURT (IN BAKING)	1 cup buttermilk
SOY SAUCE	teriyaki sauce
1 TSP. BAKING POWDER	1/2 tsp. baking soda + 1/2 tsp. cream of tartar
1 TSP. BAKING POWDER	1/4 tsp. baking soda + 1/2 cup sour milk (count as liquid in recipe)
1 CUP LIGHT CORN SYRUP	1 1/4 cup sugar + 1/3 cup liquid
1 CUP HONEY	1 1/4 cup sugar + 1/3 cup liquid
1 CUP SUGAR	1 cup packed brown sugar or 2 cups powdered sugar

RECIPE CALLS FOR:	TRY THIS INSTEAD:
1/8 TSP. CAYENNE PEPPER	3-4 drops hot pepper seasoning
1 CUP YOGURT (IN BAKING)	1 cup milk + 1 Tbsp. lemon juice or vinegar (let stand 5 minutes)
1 CUP SOUR CREAM (IN BAKING)	1 cup milk + 1 Tbsp. lemon or vinegar (let stand 5 minutes)
1 CUP BROTH	1 cup boiling water + 1 tsp. bouillon powder or 1 bouillon cube
2 CUPS TOMATO SAUCE	3/4 cup tomato paste + 1 cup water
1 CUP TOMATO JUICE	1/2 cup tomato sauce + 1/2 cup water
NONSTICK COOKING SPRAY	1/4 tsp. oil spread over pan surface

Life and Time Savers for Holidays

◆ What time of day are you most energetic? Plan and prepare for holidays at that time.

◆ Never dwell on failures. So you didn't find the perfect gift for the birthday—focus on how thankful you are just to be together to celebrate. That's the important part.

◆ Stock up on a variety of greeting cards for holidays, birthdays, and anniversaries. Keep a supply at your desk for last-minute remembrances.

◆ When loading the dishwasher, group knives, forks, and spoons together in the silverware container to save sorting time once they are clean.

◆ Pour salt on oven spills that are too hot to clean up. The job will be easier once the spot has cooled.

◆ Don't allow meaningless phone calls to interrupt your holiday preparations. Use an answering machine and return important calls at a convenient time.

◆ Trade holiday chores with a friend who has different likes and abilities.

◆ When picking up the house, carry a large basket just to pick up clutter, and redistribute things to their proper places as you travel between rooms.

◆ Make errand time efficient. When stopping at the florist to pick up fresh flowers, consider an upcoming birthday need and inquire about special promotions.

◆ If bagging your own groceries, group like items in the same sack.

◆ Attach a long cord to your kitchen phone. Cook or clean while you return or make calls.

◆ Did your pie crust flop? Blend 3 Tbsp. soft margarine, 1 Tbsp. sugar, and 1 1/4 cup graham cracker crumbs in a microproof, 9-inch pie plate. Microwave, uncovered, on high for 2 minutes. Stir crumbs, then press evenly onto the sides and bottom of a pie plate. Microwave on high 2 minutes more, rotating once. Cool before adding prepared filling.

◆ Is your brown sugar hard? Microwave a package of brown sugar on high for 15 seconds or until soft. Be careful not to let sugar liquefy.

◆ Do you hate making pies? Disguise one from the bakery with one of these toppings:

Fold 3 Tbsp. sifted powdered sugar into 2 cups reduced-fat whipped topping. Then add one of the following: 2 tsp. finely shredded orange peel, 1 Tbsp. almond liqueur, 1 Tbsp. rum, or 1/2 tsp. ground ginger, cinnamon, or cloves.

Or, fold 2 Tbsp. granulated sugar into 1 cup nonfat sour cream. Then add one of the following: 2 Tbsp. bourbon or 2 tsp. finely grated lemon or lime peel.

Table Blessings

At most holiday gatherings, there is an appropriate pause before the feasting begins—when all are standing around the buffet table with plates in hand, or when bowls are steaming and everyone is prepared to be seated. There may be a traditional family prayer of thanks that fits your holiday gathering.

William Shore, executive director of Share Our Strength, a hunger-relief organization, explains giving thanks before a meal in this way, "I've always viewed mealtime as a humbling moment. . . the need to eat unites us all and underscores a basic human frailty. It's almost as if nature had created an infallible way to remind us, daily and nearly hourly, that we are bound to and dependent upon every other living thing in this universe, a knowledge that is surely the ultimate blessing."

In my family, we use the familiar "Come Lord Jesus, be our guest, and let these gifts to us be blessed. Amen." In my husband's family (many of whom were blessed with beautiful voices) we may sing the Doxology: "Praise God from whom all blessings flow, praise him all creatures here below, praise him above ye heavenly hosts, praise Father, Son, and Holy Ghost."

My friends of Catholic faith use this prayer with hand signs: "In the name of the Father (touch forehead) and of the Son (touch chest) and of the Holy Spirit (touch left shoulder, then right shoulder). Amen. Bless us, oh Lord, in these thy gifts which we are about to receive from thy bounty through Christ our Lord.

Amen." Then sign again with or without the name words.

Whatever your heritage, a tone of thankfulness is set by offering a table blessing. Some other blessings follow:

"May your life be like a wildflower, growing freely in the beauty and joy of each day."—Native American proverb

"To see the world in a grain of sand and a heaven in a wildflower, hold infinity in the palm of your hand and eternity in an hour." —William Blake

"There are two ways to live our lives. . .one is as though nothing is a miracle. The other is as though everything is a miracle. Today we celebrate the miracle."—Albert Einstein

"He or she who knows that enough is enough will always have enough. May we learn to be grateful for whatever we have so that it may always be enough."—Chinese sage Lao Tzu

"In the end, the love you take is equal to the love you make."—Paul McCartney

For additional blessings—refer to *A Grateful Heart—Daily Blessings for the Evening Meal From Buddha to the Beatles,* by M.J. Ryan, published by Conari Press ($14.95). This collection offers a wide variety of spiritual disciplines and secular perspectives that fit anyone's needs.

Food Safety First

Holiday picnics and potlucks unfortunately often include an invitation to food-borne illness. Use these safe food handling techniques:

◆ *Cleanliness is essential. Wash hands and work areas; be sure all utensils are clean before preparing food.*

◆ *Use an insulated cooler with sufficient ice or ice packs to keep the food at 40 degrees. If you are planning on take-out foods from the deli, eat them within two hours of pickup or buy them ahead of time and chill thoroughly before packing in the cooler.*

◆ *On a hot day, place the cooler in the air-conditioned car, instead of the trunk. At the potluck, keep the cooler in the coolest place possible and replenish the ice as it melts.*

◆ *If handling raw meat, remove it from the cooler just as you are about to put it on the grill.*

To be sure bacteria are destroyed, cook hamburgers and ribs to 160 degrees and poultry to 180 degrees. When taking food off the grill, don't put cooked items on the same platter that held raw meat.

Grilling Techniques

Summer holidays revolve around the outdoor grill. The sizzle and snap of your favorite cut of meat makes your mouth water. In fact, the Fourth of July is America's number one grilling day with approximately 80 percent of the country firing up.

Reinvent the steak or chicken breast with these simple marinades and meat rubs:

FAVORITE RED MEAT MARINADE

2 Tbsp. reduced sodium soy sauce
1 Tbsp. minced fresh ginger
1 Tbsp. lemon zest
2 tsp. vegetable oil

1 clove garlic, minced
1 tsp. black pepper
1 tsp. brown sugar

Mix ingredients and marinate meat for a minimum of 15 minutes to add flavor or as long as overnight to tenderize. Always marinate in the refrigerator and discard leftover marinades that have been in contact with raw meat.

Other quick marinades:

REDUCED FAT ZESTY ITALIAN SALAD DRESSING

REDUCED FAT RED WINE VINEGAR DRESSING

REDUCED FAT WESTERN® DRESSING MIXED WITH EQUAL PARTS BEER

DRY ONION SOUP MIX COMBINED WITH BEER OR RED WINE

SALSA MIXED WITH BEER OR RED WINE

Instead of a barbecue sauce, spice up your meat for barbecue with one of these rubs:

RED MEAT RUB

1 Tbsp. each fresh or 1 tsp. each-dried:

    thyme
    rosemary
    sage
    marjoram

1 Tbsp. chopped garlic
1/2 tsp. salt
1/2 tsp. black pepper

VARIATION FOR FISH: Add grated zest of 1 lemon.

CHICKEN RUB

1 Tbsp. salt
1 Tbsp. white sugar
1 Tbsp. brown sugar
1 Tbsp. cumin
1 1/2 tsp. chili powder

1 1/2 tsp. black pepper
1 1/2 tsp. cayenne pepper
1 Tbsp. + 1 1/2 tsp. paprika
1 Tbsp. oregano

GINGER RUB FOR CHICKEN OR FISH

4 Tbsp. minced fresh ginger root   3 Tbsp. lemon juice
2 Tbsp. minced garlic   1 tsp. ground thyme

RUB FOR BLACKENED MEATS

1 Tbsp. black pepper   1 tsp. onion powder
1 Tbsp. white pepper   1/2 tsp. celery salt
2 tsp. paprika   1 tsp. rosemary
1 tsp. granulated garlic or garlic
powder

What to Do With Leftovers

Whatever you have too much of, you can recycle it.

◆ *Is there extra turkey stuffing? Add some cooked turkey and stir-fry in a skillet for supper the next night.*

◆ *Use leftover gravy by adding cooked meat and a favorite vegetable. Then serve over mashed potatoes or toast.*

◆ *Add leftover rice to a can of soup or make a rice salad with finely chopped onion and celery, chopped turkey or ham, and a reduced-fat dressing.*

◆ *Do you have mashed potatoes coming out the ears? Add them to the bread machine for potato bread, or make a cream of potato soup. Or spoon potatoes onto a baking sheet, sprinkle with Parmesan cheese, and bake in a 400-degree oven until slightly browned (about 15 minutes).*

◆ *Is your fresh fruit salad turning brown? Douse it with a 12-ounce can of sugar-free lemon lime soft drink or 1 1/2 cups cran-raspberry juice, then ladle into 8-ounce plastic cups and freeze. To serve, microcook on high power for 45 seconds and enjoy a fruit slush.*

◆ *Any leftover vegetable can find its way into a batch of soup or chef's salad.*

Freeze Leftovers Right

You'll be happy to greet those leftovers next week or next month when you need a quick meal. The appropriate wrapping ensures almost-fresh flavor and prevents freezer burn. The term freezer burn is contradictory, but describes what happens to food when it is exposed to extreme cold. The food usually discolors and dries out on the surface. The best freezer materials are moisture- and vapor-proof, durable, and resistant to oil and grease, and easy to label.

ALUMINUM FOIL: Use heavy-duty rather than regular foil for better protection. Mold the foil to the shape of the food and take care not to puncture it. Avoid using foil to wrap foods that contain acid, such as tomatoes. Acid reacts with the aluminum, giving the food an off-flavor.

FREEZER PLASTIC WRAP: Clear plastic freezer wrap is heavier than everyday plastic wrap.

BAKING DISHES: Use dishes that are recommended for freezer-to-oven or freezer-to-microwave use.

PLASTIC CONTAINERS: These work well if fitted with a tight lid.

The following materials are not moisture- and vapor-proof:

> Aluminum foil other than heavy-duty
>
> Waxed paper not labeled for freezer use
>
> Plastic wrap not labeled for freezer use
>
> Glass jars not recommended for freezing
>
> Pottery
>
> Nonflexible plastic
>
> Plastic bags not labeled as freezer bags

Time Table for Safe Storage

HOLIDAY FOOD	SAFE DAYS IN REFRIGERATOR	SAFE MONTHS IN FREEZER
Deboned turkey/gravy	3-4	4
Turkey, no gravy	1-2	6
Ham slices	3-4	1-2
Stuffing	1-2	2-3
Cranberry sauce	7	—

HOLIDAY FOOD	SAFE DAYS IN REFRIGERATOR	SAFE MONTHS IN FREEZER
Mashed potatoes	3-4	—
Pumpkin pie	3-4	1-2
Grilled meat	1-2	—
Roasted meat	3-4	1-2
Breads or rolls	6	3
Vegetable salads	1-2	—
Cooked vegetables	1-2	1
Mixed fresh fruit	1	1

> ### Remember the Time . . .
> ### Snubbing TV for Family Games

When kids are asked about their favorite holiday memory, they usually recite some silly family story like the time "Grandma played hide and seek with us and got stuck in the closet." Create fun at your next holiday gathering by turning off the TV and tuning into each other. Some ideas for family games follow:

LAUGHTER CHAIN REACTION

Unleash uncontrollable laughter in your living room. You need at least three people (big or little). One person lies down on the floor. A second puts his or her head on the first person's stomach. A third then puts his or her head on the second's stomach and so on. The first person says "ha" after which the second says "ha, ha" and so on around the room. Eventually, the "ha's" turn into genuine laughter. To test willpower, see how long everybody can maintain their positions without laughing. See who holds out the longest.

QUARTER TOSS

Line the children up in a row, and assign someone to be the judge. Ask each child to toss a quarter as high as they can and catch it in the palm of the hand before it strikes anything else. The judge decides who the winner is by who flipped the coin the highest. The winner gets to keep the quarter.

FAMILY OLYMPICS

Divide the active members of your family up into two teams. Set up start and finish lines, then choose from these relay events:

—hop on one foot on a 20' stretch of yarn.

—walk backwards while flapping your arms.

—crawl on all fours while balancing a book on your head.

FAMILY CHRONICLE

This activity is meant for an extended visit, such as a three-day weekend holiday. Gather some scratch paper, and let the kids write a family newspaper. The adults can write stories as told by the younger children, and the older children can write their own stories. Ask Grandpa what holiday celebrations were like when he was a kid, or ask the children to tell about their favorite toys at Grandma's house. Describe favorite family recipes, or predict who's going to win the Rose Bowl.

FOX AND GOOSE

Fresh winter snow is needed for this game. First, make a course by stomping out a circle 20 feet in diameter into the snow. Next, make six paths that cross at the center, dividing the circle into a pie. One person plays the fox and the other the goose. The fox can chase and try to tag the goose, always following the tromped down circle and pathways. Upon tagging the goose, the goose becomes the fox and a new person is selected to be the goose.

WATER BALLOON TOSS

For a summer holiday, plan an afternoon balloon toss. Purchase some good quality medium-size balloons. Fill them with water, tie the ends and store them in a five-gallon plastic pail. Divide the group up into pairs. Line the group up with each pair facing each other. Give each pair one balloon. On the count of three, they toss the balloon to the partner. The leader then instructs everybody to take one step back. They toss the balloon again. Keep tossing and stepping back until all of the balloons except one have been broken. The pair that hasn't broken their balloon is the winner.

WHAT'S IN MY POCKET?

The first person says, "My pocket is so heavy because it holds a Great Dane. The second person says, "My pocket is so heavy because it holds a Great Dane, and a bath tub." The third person says, "My pocket is so heavy because it holds a Great Dane, a bath tub, and an apple pie." Continue around the group until someone flubs!

GOOD DAY!

This game is intended for school-age children who arrive before the other guests. Teach each child how to say "Good day" in another language. They can greet the visitors as they arrive with a foreign greeting:

CHINESE: *Neehow (Knee how)*

DUTCH: *Goeden dag (Gooden daug)*

FRENCH: *Bonjour (Bone jour)*

GERMAN: *Guten tag (Gooten togg)*

HEBREW: *Shalom (Shah lome)*

JAPANESE: *Konichee-wa (Cone ee chee wah)*

SPANISH: *Buenos dias (Bway nos dee us)*

EASY OUTDOOR GAMES:

Set up an obstacle course

Hopscotch

Potato Sack Relays (use an old pillowcase)

Freeze Tag

Hide and Seek

OTHER EASY INDOOR GAMES

Charades

Arm Wrestling

Telephone

Thumb Wrestling

Button, Button, Who's Got the Button?

TIME TO CLEAN UP AND GO HOME GAME

Divide the adults and children into groups. Assign each group a room or area to pick up or clean up before the party ends. Set the kitchen timer for five minutes. See which group gets done first.

For additional ideas, consult the book *365 TV-Free Activities*, by Steve and Ruth Bennett, published by Bob Adams, Inc., Holbrook, Massachusetts ($6.25).

NEW YEAR'S DAY

Significant Symbols

CHANGE AND RENEWAL

January 1, New Year's Day, is a celebration of starting over, of wiping the slate clean and starting something fresh. Favorite and comforting foods are the menu for the day. Swedes eat cabbage, Scots eat shortbread, and Italians eat lentils. Do you like to make New Year's resolutions? Make one simple measurable obtainable resolution and write it down or record it in some way. Keep the written record or tape until next New Year's.

PARADES AND FOOTBALL

In our culture, New Year's Day parades and college football bowl games have become tradition. Tailgate activities take over living rooms across the nation.

ADD FUN, SUBTRACT EXPENSE

◆ *If you have snow, have a snow sculpture festival on New Year's Day.*

◆ *Adopt the old European custom of making a pilgrimage on New Year's Day. Visit friends or relatives, or call long-distance friends while the rate is low.*

◆ *If football isn't your fancy, rent a favorite movie from the previous year. Make your Oscar nomination predictions.*

◆ *Use New Year's Day to send cards if December finds your Christmas cards still in the box. Eliminate one activity that causes stress before Christmas. Friends receiving New Year's cards will have more time to appreciate them as well.*

MENU IDEAS

NEW YEAR'S PARADE BRUNCH

Cranberry Cooler

No-Fuss Ground Pork Lasagna or Broccoli Breakfast Pie

Mixed Greens with Shredded Red Cabbage and Low-Fat Celery Seed Dressing

Lemon Creme with Fresh Fruit Dippers

BOWL DAY BUFFET

Sloppy Joe Squares

Taco Dip with Low-Fat Tortilla Chips

Herb Cheese Spread with Low-Fat Crackers and Carrot and Celery Dippers

Grasshopper Pie

TAKE DOWN THE CHRISTMAS TREE SUPPER

Hot Potato Buffet

Bacon Ranch Dip with Broccoli and Cauliflower Dippers

Espresso Nut Mousse

CRANBERRY COOLER

FAT-FREE!

Serves 8, 6 oz. each
A thirst-quenching favorite for New Year's Day.

12-oz. can frozen cran-raspberry
or cranberry juice cocktail

3 12-oz. cans lemon or raspberry
flavored mineral water

10 ice cubes

Combine all ingredients in a 3-quart pitcher and serve immediately to sustain fizz. Garnish the pitcher with a twisted slice of lemon rind. For brunches, serve in a stemmed wine glass. Kids love to drink this out of a short, fat tumbler.

NUTRIENTS PER SERVING

*102 calories, 0 fat, 0 saturated fat, 0 cholesterol, 6 mg. sodium,
26 gm. carbohydrate, 0 protein*

Count as 1 1/2 fruit for food exchange eating plans.

5 minutes "hands-on" preparation time

NO-FUSS GROUND PORK LASAGNA

Serves 15, brunch-size portions

1 lb. lean ground pork

1/4 tsp. salt

28-oz. jar reduced-fat spaghetti sauce

14-oz. can Italian-style diced tomatoes, undrained

1/4 tsp. ground red pepper

1 egg or 1/4 cup liquid egg substitute

15 oz. fat-free ricotta cheese

1/4 cup grated Parmesan cheese

10 uncooked lasagna noodles

4 oz. part-skim mozzarella cheese, shredded

OPTIONAL GARNISH: Layer three fresh spinach leaves on a dinner plate, and serve lasagna on top of them.

Preheat oven to 375° F. In a large skillet, brown ground pork with salt over medium heat for 5 to 10 minutes, until cooked through. Drain pork in a colander and return it to the skillet. Stir in spaghetti sauce, tomatoes, and red pepper, and set aside. Meanwhile, in a medium bowl, beat egg until smooth; stir in ricotta and Parmesan cheese. Spread 2 cups of pork mixture over the bottom of a 9- by 13-inch pan. Arrange 4 lasagna noodles lengthwise in a single layer over the pork. Place the 5th noodle across the end of the baking dish. Spread entire ricotta cheese mixture over the noodles. Sprinkle with half of the mozzarella cheese. Pour half of remaining pork mixture over the cheese. Press remaining noodles on top. Pour remaining pork mixture over the cheese. Cover with foil and bake for 45 minutes. Remove foil and sprinkle with remaining mozzarella cheese. Return lasagna, uncovered, to the oven for 5 minutes. Remove from the oven and allow to stand 10 minutes at room temperature before cutting into 5 rows, 3 squares per row.

NUTRIENTS PER SERVING

*195 calories, 6 gm. fat, 2 gm. saturated fat, 43 mg. cholesterol with egg
(29 mg. with egg sub.), 514 mg. sodium, 21 gm. carbohydrate, 17 gm. protein*

*Count as 1 bread/starch, 1 vegetable, and 1 1/2 lean meat
for food exchange eating plans.*

20 minutes "hands-on" preparation time, 60 minutes baking time

BROCCOLI BREAKFAST PIE

Serves 8

1 bunch fresh broccoli,
  flowerets only

1 cup cooked, diced chicken

1 medium yellow onion, chopped

4 oz. reduced-fat cheddar cheese,
  shredded

1 1/3 cup skim milk

3 eggs or 3/4 cup liquid egg
  substitute

3/4 cup reduced-fat baking mix
  (such as Bisquick® Light)

1/4 tsp. salt

1/4 tsp. pepper

1/2 tsp. curry powder

OPTIONAL GARNISH:
  red pepper flakes

Preheat oven to 400° F. Spray a large (10-inch) pie pan with non-stick cooking spray. Layer first four ingredients in the pan. In a blender container, combine remaining ingredients. Blend on medium speed for 30 seconds or until mixture is smooth. Pour egg mixture into the pan. **OPTIONAL GARNISH:** sprinkle red pepper flakes on the top of the egg mixture. Bake for 25 to 30 minutes until firm. Allow pie to sit at room temperature for 10 minutes before slicing. This recipe may be assembled a day ahead and refrigerated overnight. Increase baking time to 35 minutes for chilled mixture.

NUTRIENTS PER SERVING

226 calories, 6 gm. fat, 2 gm. saturated fat, 107 mg. cholesterol with egg (27 mg. with egg sub.), 570 mg. sodium, 22 gm. carbohydrate, 21 gm. protein

Count as 1 bread/starch, 1 vegetable, and 2 1/2 lean meat for food exchange eating plans.

15 minutes "hands-on" preparation time, 30 minutes baking time

LOW-FAT CELERY SEED DRESSING
ONLY 3 GRAMS OF FAT

Serves 8, 2 Tbsp. each

1/2 cup sugar
1/3 cup vinegar
2 Tbsp. finely-grated white onion
1 tsp. dry mustard

1/8 cup vegetable oil
1 1/2 Tbsp. celery seed

Combine all ingredients in a shaker container. Serve over fresh greens mixed with shredded red cabbage.

NUTRIENTS PER SERVING

79 calories, 3 gm. fat, 0 saturated fat, 0 cholesterol, 0 sodium, 13 gm. carbohydrate, 0 protein

Count as 1 fruit and 1/2 fat for food exchange eating plans.

5 minutes "hands-on" preparation time

LEMON CREME WITH FRESH FRUIT DIPPERS

Serves 8, 1/4 cup each

1 cup fat-free ricotta cheese	2 Tbsp. finely grated lemon rind
3 Tbsp. powdered sugar	1 cup reduced-fat whipped topping

In a blender container, process ricotta cheese with powdered sugar. Turn out into a 1-quart glass bowl. Fold in lemon rind and whipped topping. Place bowl in the middle of a serving plate and decorate outside of plate with red apple and yellow pear slices, chunks of pineapple, and fresh green grapes.

NUTRIENTS PER SERVING

107 calories, 5 gm. fat, 2 gm. saturated fat, 3 mg. cholesterol, 15 mg. sodium, 15 gm. carbohydrate, 4 gm. protein

Count as 1/2 skim milk, 1/2 fruit, and 1 fat for food exchange eating plans.

15 minutes "hands-on" preparation time

SLOPPY JOE SQUARES

Serves 12

1 lb. lean ground beef	1 cup skim milk
15-oz. can sloppy joe sauce	2 cups reduced-fat baking mix, such as Bisquick® light)
4 oz. reduced-fat cheddar cheese, shredded	2 Tbsp. sesame seeds
2 eggs or 1/2 cup liquid egg substitute	

Preheat oven to 400° F. In a medium skillet, brown ground beef. Drain in a colander. Return beef to the skillet and stir in sauce. Spoon meat and sauce into a 9- by 13-inch pan that has been sprayed with nonstick cooking spray. Sprinkle cheese over the meat. In a medium mixing bowl, beat eggs until smooth, then stir in milk and baking mix. Pour egg mixture over the cheese. Sprinkle with sesame seeds. Bake for 30 minutes or until crust is lightly browned. Cut into 4 rows, 3 squares each. Use a short metal spatula to remove squares from the pan.

NUTRIENTS PER SERVING

263 calories, 10 gm. fat, 3 gm. saturated fat, 66 mg. cholesterol with egg (31 mg. with egg sub.), 648 mg. sodium, 26 gm. carbohydrate, 15 gm. protein

Count as 2 bread/starch, 1 lean meat, and 1 fat for food exchange eating plans.

15 minutes "hands-on" preparation time, 30 minutes baking time

TACO DIP

ONLY 2 GRAMS OF FAT

Serves 8, 1/2 cup each

16-oz. can refried beans
1 cup medium salsa
8 oz. nonfat sour cream

2 oz. reduced-fat Monterey Jack cheese, shredded
Reduced-fat chips such as baked Tostitos®

Combine refried beans with salsa in a mixing bowl. Cover with plastic wrap and microcook on high power for 4 minutes. Turn beans out onto a 10-inch pie plate. Cover with sour cream, then sprinkle with shredded cheese. Keep pie plate warm on a warming tray. Serve with reduced-fat tortilla chips.

NUTRIENTS PER SERVING

110 calories, 2 gm. fat, 1 gm. saturated fat, 5 mg. cholesterol, 624 mg. sodium, 17 gm. carbohydrate, 8 gm. protein

Count as 1 bread/starch and 1/2 skim milk for food exchange eating plans.

10 minutes "hands-on" preparation time, 5 minutes cooking time

HERB CHEESE SPREAD

ONLY 3 GRAMS OF FAT

Serves 16, 2 Tbsp. each

8 oz. reduced-fat cream cheese, softened

8 oz. reduced-fat soft processed cheddar cheese
(such as Spreadery by Kraft®)

2 Tbsp. skim milk

2 Tbsp. lemon juice

1/2 tsp. basil

1/2 tsp. oregano

1/2 tsp. marjoram

1/2 tsp. thyme

1/4 tsp. garlic powder

Crackers, pretzels, vegetables

Preheat oven to 350° F. In a medium mixing bowl, beat cheeses together just until smooth, then gradually beat in milk, and then beat in lemon juice. Stir in remaining ingredients. Turn into an 9-inch pie plate. Bake for 15 minutes. Serve hot cheese dip with reduced fat crackers such as Harvest Crisps®, pretzels, or fresh carrot and celery sticks.

NUTRIENTS PER SERVING

50 calories, 3 gm. fat, 1 gm. saturated fat, 10 mg. cholesterol, 277 mg. sodium, 2 gm. carbohydrate, 3 gm. protein

Count as 1 fat for food exchange eating plans.

10 minutes "hands-on" preparation time, 15 minutes baking time

GRASSHOPPER PIE

Serves 8

1 cup lime sherbet, softened

2 cups vanilla frozen yogurt, softened

1 1/2 cups reduced-fat whipped topping

2 Tbsp. creme de menthe or 1 Tbsp. green peppermint extract

OPTIONAL: 1 Tbsp. creme de cacao

9-inch prepared chocolate cookie crust

OPTIONAL GARNISH: crushed peppermint candy or finely grated chocolate

In a large mixing bowl, gently fold first 5 ingredients together until blended. Pour into crust and freeze at least 4 hours before serving. Garnish the top with crushed peppermint candy or finely grated chocolate.

NUTRIENTS PER SERVING

244 calories, 7 gm. fat, 2 gm. saturated fat, 2 mg. cholesterol, 180 mg. sodium, 43 gm. carbohydrate, 3 gm. protein

Count as 2 bread/starch, 1/2 fruit, and 1 fat for food exchange eating plans.

15 minutes "hands-on" preparation time, 4 hours freezing time

HOT POTATO BUFFET

ONLY 2 GRAMS OF FAT

Serves 8

8 baking potatoes, scrubbed clean

TOPPINGS:

1 cup frozen peas, thawed
1/2 cup shredded red onion
1/2 cup sliced mushrooms
8 oz. lean ham, cubed
1 cup nonfat sour cream
1/4 cup chopped fresh chives

Preheat oven to 425° F. Bake potatoes for 1 hour, then test with a fork for tenderness. Meanwhile, prepare toppings, arranging peas, onion, mushrooms, and ham on a divided relish plate or large platter. Serve baked potatoes in a basket and allow diners to decorate their potato with toppings.

NUTRIENTS PER SERVING

210 calories, 2 gm. fat, 1 gm. saturated fat, 42 mg. cholesterol, 438 mg. sodium, 36 gm. carbohydrate, 12 gm. protein

Count as 1 1/2 bread/starch, 1 lean meat, and 1 vegetable for food exchange eating plans.

15 minutes "hands-on" preparation time, 60 minutes baking time

BACON RANCH DIP

Serves 8, 2 Tbsp. each

2 strips bacon, diced   1/3 cup nonfat sour cream
2/3 cup reduced-fat Hidden
  Valley Ranch salad dressing

In a small skillet, cook diced bacon until crisp. Drain well. In a small bowl, mix salad dressing and sour cream until smooth, then fold in bacon. Refrigerate and serve with cauliflower and broccoli for dippers.

NUTRIENTS PER SERVING

56 calories, 5 gm. fat, 0 saturated fat, 8 mg. cholesterol, 225 mg. sodium, 3 gm. carbohydrate, 1 gm. protein

Count as 1 fat for food exchange eating plans.

10 minutes "hands-on" preparation time

ESPRESSO NUT MOUSSE

Serves 4, 1/2 cup each

1 pkg. milk chocolate mousse mix
  (such as Knorr®)

Skim milk

2 Tbsp. instant coffee powder

2 Tbsp. hot water

2 Tbsp. slivered almonds

Prepare mousse mix with skim milk as directed. In a glass cup measure, dissolve coffee powder in hot water. Fold coffee into mousse. Spoon into dessert dishes and garnish with slivered almonds. Refrigerate at least 2 hours.

NUTRIENTS PER SERVING

109 calories, 4 gm. fat, 1 gm. saturated fat, 2 mg. cholesterol, 69 mg. sodium, 13 gm. carbohydrate, 6 gm. protein

Count as 1 skim milk and 1/2 fat for food exchange eating plans.

15 minutes "hands-on" preparation time, 2 hours chilling time

MARTIN LUTHER KING, JR.'S BIRTHDAY

Significant Symbols

REFLECTION

Martin Luther King, Jr.'s birthday, January 20, is celebrated on the third Monday of January. The holiday encourages reflection on the life and accomplishments of the leader of the civil rights movement in our country. Martin Luther King, Jr. was a good cook, according to the biography (My *Life with Martin Luther King, Jr.*) written by his wife, Coretta Scott King. It was his turn to cook every Thursday night, and he preferred turnip greens with ham and bacon, cabbage, pork chops, fried chicken, and cornbread from a mix. Discover the highly seasoned, overcooked taste of southern soul food on King's birthday.

ADD FUN, SUBTRACT EXPENSE

◆ *Take time to read about Martin Luther King, Jr. His birthday is marked annually by stories in the daily newspaper and on television news.*

◆ *Check out one of the books he wrote from your local library.*

◆ *Take time to explain to your children the remarkable passage we have made from the 60s marches and segregated schools.*

MENU IDEAS

Pork Chops with Smothered Cabbage or Crispy Coated Chicken

Skillet Succotash or Southern Style Turnip Greens

One-Bowl Spoonbread with Honey

Confetti Coleslaw

Bread Pudding with Raisin Sauce or
Sweet Potato Custard

PORK CHOPS WITH SMOTHERED CABBAGE

Serves 4

4 lean 3-oz. pork chops
1/2 tsp. pepper
1/8 tsp. salt

16-oz. can sauerkraut or 4 cups grated fresh cabbage
1 fresh potato, grated

Preheat oven to 350° F. In a medium skillet, brown pork chops over medium heat. Season with salt and pepper. Meanwhile, in an 11- by 7-inch baking dish, combine sauerkraut or fresh cabbage with grated potato. Use a spoon to spread mixture evenly over the bottom of the dish. Arrange browned chops on top of the kraut mixture. Cover and bake for 1 hour.

NUTRIENTS PER SERVING

*287 calories, 11 gm. fat, 4 gm. saturated fat, 72 mg. cholesterol,
865 mg. sodium (to reduce sodium, choose cabbage instead of
sauerkraut), 17 gm. carbohydrate, 30 gm. protein*

Count as 3 vegetable and 3 lean meat for food exchange eating plans.

15 minutes "hands-on" preparation time, 60 minutes baking time

CRISPY COATED CHICKEN

ONLY 3 GRAMS OF FAT

Serves 8

8 boneless, skinless chicken
  breasts
1/2 cup unseasoned bread crumbs

1 oz. packet Hidden Valley
  Ranch original
  dry salad dressing mix

Preheat oven to 375° F. Combine bread crumbs and dressing mix
in a plastic bag. Add chicken breasts and shake until well coated.
Place on a baking sheet and bake for 35 to 45 minutes.

NUTRIENTS PER SERVING

*176 calories, 3 gm. fat, 1 gm. saturated fat, 73 mg. cholesterol,
522 mg. sodium, 7 gm. carbohydrate, 28 gm. protein*

Count as 3 lean meat for food exchange eating plans.

10 minutes "hands-on" preparation time, 45 minutes baking time

SKILLET SUCCOTASH
ONLY 2 GRAMS OF FAT

Serves 8, 2/3 cup each

1 tsp. vegetable oil

1 medium yellow onion, chopped fine

16-oz. can whole kernel corn, well drained

16-oz. can lima beans, well drained

1 cup canned chunky tomatoes with green chiles

1 Tbsp. butter-flavored sprinkles

1/4 tsp. black pepper

Heat oil in a large skillet, then add onions and sauté for 3 minutes. Add remaining ingredients and cover. Simmer over medium-low heat for 10 minutes.

NUTRIENTS PER SERVING

98 calories, 2 gm. fat, 0 saturated fat, 0 cholesterol, 322 mg. sodium, 16 gm. carbohydrate, 4 gm. protein

Count as 1 vegetable and 1 bread/starch for food exchange eating plans.

10 minutes "hands-on" preparation time, 15 minutes cooking time

SOUTHERN STYLE GREENS
ONLY 2 GRAMS OF FAT

Serves 8, 1 cup each

4 lb. collard, turnip or mustard greens, washed

1 cup boiling water

1/2 tsp. salt

1/4 tsp. pepper

2 Tbsp. white vinegar

2 Tbsp. reduced-fat butter-flavored margarine such as I Can't Believe It's Not Butter®

Break greens into small pieces or chop fine. Place greens in a large pot, add water and salt. Cover and simmer over medium-low heat for 15 minutes. Drain and stir in pepper, vinegar, and margarine.

NUTRIENTS PER SERVING

88 calories, 2 gm. fat, 0 saturated fat, 0 cholesterol, 82 mg. sodium, 16 gm. carbohydrate, 3 gm. protein

Count as 3 vegetable and 1/2 fat for food exchange eating plans.

10 minutes "hands-on" preparation time, 15 minutes cooking time

ONE BOWL SPOON BREAD WITH HONEY

ONLY 3 GRAMS OF FAT

Serves 16, 1/2 cup each

14-oz. can evaporated skim milk

1/3 cup skim milk

2 Tbsp. margarine

2 Tbsp. sugar

1 tsp. salt

1 cup cornmeal

1 tsp. baking powder

4 eggs or 1 cup liquid egg substitute

TOPPINGS:
salt, pepper, reduced-fat margarine, honey

Preheat oven to 375° F. In a medium pan, heat evaporated skim milk, skim milk, margarine, sugar, and salt uncovered over medium heat until scalding. Remove from heat and mix in cornmeal, beating smooth. Add eggs or egg substitute, beating mixture well. Turn out into a 2-quart casserole dish that has been sprayed with nonstick cooking spray. Bake for 30 minutes until lightly browned. Serve spoon bread just out of the oven with extra salt, pepper, reduced-fat margarine, and honey.

CONFETTI COLESLAW

ONLY 3 GRAMS OF FAT

Serves 8, 1 cup each

1 lb. fresh cabbage, coarsely shredded, or 1-lb. bag pre-shredded cabbage

1 large tomato, seeded and diced

1 large green pepper, diced

3 green onions, finely chopped

1/2 cup lemon juice

1/3 cup sugar

2 Tbsp. vegetable oil

1 tsp. salt

1/2 tsp. dry mustard

In a salad bowl, combine cabbage, tomato, pepper, and onions. In a small saucepan, combine remaining ingredients. Bring mixture to a boil and pour over vegetables. Cover and chill overnight or at least 3 hours to blend flavors.

BREAD PUDDING WITH RAISIN SAUCE

ONLY 2 GRAMS OF FAT

Serves 12

4 cups white bread cubes (8 slices)
4 eggs, slightly beaten or 1 cup
  liquid egg substitute

2 3/4 cups skim milk
1/2 cup packed brown sugar
2 tsp. cinnamon

Preheat oven to 350° F. Arrange bread cubes in a 9-inch square baking pan that has been sprayed with nonstick cooking spray. In a medium bowl, combine eggs, milk, sugar, and cinnamon. Beat well, and pour over bread. Bake for 45 minutes or until knife inserted near center comes out clean. Meanwhile, prepare sauce.

RAISIN SAUCE:

1/2 cup sugar
1/4 cup brown sugar
2 Tbsp. cornstarch
3/4 cup water

1/4 cup orange juice
1/4 cup raisins
1 Tbsp. reduced-fat margarine

In a small saucepan, combine sugars and cornstarch. Gradually add water and orange juice. Mix well. Over medium heat, cook and stir mixture until boiling. Reduce heat to low, cook for 3 minutes or until clear. Stir in raisins and margarine. Serve warm over bread pudding.

NUTRIENTS PER SERVING

189 calories, 2 gm. fat, 0 saturated fat, 71 mg. cholesterol with egg (1 mg. with egg sub.), 156 mg. sodium, 35 gm. carbohydrate, 5 gm. protein

Count as 1 1/2 fruit, 1 bread/starch, and 1/2 fat for food exchange eating plans.

20 minutes "hands-on" preparation time, 45 minutes baking time

SWEET POTATO CUSTARD

Serves 8, 1/2 cup each

2 large cooked and mashed sweet potatoes or 2 cups mashed yams or butternut squash

1/4 cup brown sugar

2 Tbsp. margarine

2 Tbsp. skim milk

3 Tbsp. flour

4 eggs, well beaten or 1 cup liquid egg substitute

1/2 tsp. cinnamon

1/4 tsp. cloves

1 Tbsp. finely grated orange rind

Combine all ingredients in a large mixing bowl. Beat until smooth. Pour into a baking dish that has been sprayed with nonstick cooking spray. Bake for 45 minutes. Serve warm with a dollop of reduced-fat whipped topping.

NUTRIENTS PER SERVING

156 calories, 4 gm. fat, 1 gm. saturated fat, 106 mg. cholesterol with egg (0 with egg sub.), 76 mg. sodium, 26 gm. carbohydrate, 4 gm. protein

Count as 1 fruit, 1 bread/starch, and 1/2 fat for food exchange eating plans.

20 minutes "hands-on" preparation time, 45 minutes baking time

Significant Symbols

ANIMALS

The 1995 Chinese New Year marked the Year of the Pig. Parades occur in the Chinese sections of our large cities and elaborately celebrate the animal theme. During festival days, Chinese people splurge on shrimp, capon, and spareribs.

ADD FUN, SUBTRACT EXPENSE

◆ *Use chopsticks instead of silverware.*

◆ *Dust off that Chinese tea pot, and use it at dessert time.*

◆ *Pick up some fortune cookies, and share your fortune with family members.*

MENU IDEAS

Spring Rolls with Mustard Sauce
Crabmeat and Cucumber Salad
Chicken with Snow Peas or Shanghai Chicken
Pears Cardinal or Pineapple Flan

SPRING ROLLS

This recipe is adapted from one shared by Kathie Bentley, who introduced spring rolls to my "Fight Winter Fat" class.
Serves 24, 1 roll each

FILLING:

1/2 lb. lean ground pork
1/2 lb. fresh bean sprouts
1 lb. shredded cabbage
1 small onion, chopped
1 sweet potato, shredded
1 tsp. MSG

1/2 tsp. pepper
1/4 cup reduced-sodium soy sauce
1 egg
24 spring roll skins or egg roll wrappers
Vegetable oil

Mix ingredients for filling in a large bowl. Place 1 Tbsp. filling mixture at one corner of the egg roll wrapper. Roll the corner up tightly to the midpoint of the triangle. Next, fold in the left and right sides of the triangle. Continue to roll up the skin. Dab the end point of the triangle with water to paste it shut. Fry spring rolls in 1 inch of 360° vegetable oil in a wok or large skillet until skin is mottled. Drain well and serve. The cooked rolls may also be frozen. Remove from freezer and bake for 10 minutes at 350° F. to freshen and crisp for later service.

NUTRIENTS PER SERVING (INCLUDES VEGETABLE OIL)

83 calories, 6 gm. fat, 0 saturated fat, 16 mg. cholesterol, 200 mg. sodium, 4 gm. carbohydrate, 3 gm. protein

Count as 1/2 bread/starch and 1 fat for food exchange eating plans.

20 minutes "hands-on" preparation time, 20 minutes cooking time

MUSTARD SAUCE FOR SPRING ROLLS

FAT-FREE!

Serves 24, 2 tsp. each

1/2 cup sugar
2 Tbsp. flour
3 Tbsp. Dijon or yellow mustard

1/4 cup herb vinegar
3/4 cup water

Combine all ingredients in a small saucepan. Use a whisk and stir over medium heat to boiling. Boil for 2 minutes, stirring continuously. Remove from heat and cool to room temperature before serving with spring rolls.

NUTRIENTS PER SERVING

22 calories, 0 fat, 0 saturated fat, 0 cholesterol, 24 mg. sodium, 5 gm. carbohydrate, 0 protein

Count as 1/2 fruit for food exchange eating plans.

10 minutes "hands-on" preparation time

CRABMEAT AND CUCUMBER SALAD

FAT-FREE!

Serves 8, 3/4 cup each

3 large cucumbers, peeled and
  sliced thin
8 oz. crab or mock crab, diced
1 Tbsp. soy sauce

2 tsp. vinegar
1 tsp. vegetable oil
1 tsp. sugar
1 tsp. minced ginger

Mix all ingredients together in a salad bowl. Marinate for 10 minutes. Serve cold.

....

NUTRIENTS PER SERVING

*46 calories, 0 fat, 0 saturated fat, 11 mg. cholesterol, 3
64 mg. sodium, 3 gm. carbohydrate, 6 gm. protein*

Count as 1 vegetable and 1/2 lean meat for food exchange eating plans.

15 minutes "hands-on" preparation time, 10 minutes chilling time

CHICKEN WITH SNOW PEAS

Serves 4, 1 cup each

2 whole chicken breasts, skinned, boned, and diced

1 egg white

1 tsp. cornstarch

1 tsp. white wine

1 Tbsp. oil

1/2 tsp. ginger

1/2 tsp. minced garlic

12 snow peas

1/2 cup chicken broth

1/4 tsp. salt

Mix diced chicken with egg white, cornstarch, and wine. Heat oil in skillet for 1 minute; add ginger and garlic and sauté for 1 minute. Add chicken and stir-fry for 4 minutes. Add snow peas, chicken broth and salt, and bring to boil, stirring mixture as it thickens. Serve over rice.

NUTRIENTS PER SERVING

*193 calories, 4 gm. fat, 1 gm. saturated fat, 73 mg. cholesterol,
375 mg. sodium, 2 gm. carbohydrate, 28 gm. protein*

Count as 3 lean meat and 1 vegetable for food exchange eating plans.

20 minutes "hands-on" preparation time, 10 minutes cooking time

SHANGHAI CHICKEN

Serves 4

1 Tbsp. vegetable oil

1/2 tsp. ginger

2 green onions, cut into 1-inch pieces

2 whole chicken breasts, skinned, boned, and diced

8 oz. fresh mushrooms, sliced thin

8-oz. can bamboo shoots, drained

1/2 cup soy sauce

1/2 cup white wine

1 Tbsp. sugar

Heat oil in a wok or skillet for 1 minute. Add ginger and green onions. Sauté for 1 minute. Add chicken, and cook for 3 to 4 minutes. Add mushrooms, bamboo shoots, soy sauce, wine, and sugar. Simmer, uncovered over low heat for 20 minutes. Serve over rice.

NUTRIENTS PER SERVING

252 calories, 6 gm. fat, 1 gm. saturated fat, 73 mg. cholesterol, 1969 mg. sodium (to reduce sodium, use reduced sodium soy sauce), 10 gm. carbohydrate, 32 gm. protein

Count as 4 lean meat and 2 vegetable for food exchange eating plans.

15 minutes "hands-on" preparation time, 20 minutes cooking time

PEARS CARDINAL

FAT-FREE!

Serves 8

4 large, firm, ripe pears

16-oz. package frozen raspberries, thawed

2 Tbsp. sugar

2 tsp. cornstarch dissolved in 2 Tbsp. water

Place pears in a steam basket over 2 inches of water. Steam over medium-high heat for 10 minutes. Gently remove pears from steamer and run under cold water, gently peeling away skin. Cover pears and refrigerate. Meanwhile, combine raspberries, sugar, and cornstarch and water mixture in a medium-size saucepan. Bring mixture to a boil. Continue to simmer for 2 minutes. Refrigerate until service. Serve pears in individual serving bowls, and spoon sauce over and around each one.

NUTRIENTS PER SERVING

129 calories, 0 fat, 0 saturated fat, 0 cholesterol, 1 mg. sodium, 33 gm. carbohydrate, 1 gm. protein

Count as 2 fruit for food exchange eating plans.

15 minutes "hands-on" preparation time, 15 minutes cooking time

PINEAPPLE FLAN

ONLY 2 GRAMS OF FAT

Serves 8, 1 small custard cup each

4 Tbsp. orange marmalade

1 cup pineapple tidbits in juice

4 maraschino cherries, cut in half

4 eggs or 1 cup liquid egg
  substitute

2/3 cup evaporated skimmed milk

1/2 cup sugar

1 tsp. vanilla

Preheat oven to 350° F. Place 1/2 Tbsp. orange marmalade in the bottom of 8 small custard baking cups. Place 2 Tbsp. of pineapple tidbits over the marmalade. Place one half cherry in the center of the pineapple slice. In a medium-size mixing bowl, beat eggs with milk, sugar, and vanilla until well blended. Fill each cup with mixture. Place dishes in a shallow baking pan that has been filled with water. Bake for 30 minutes or until custard is firm.

NUTRIENTS PER SERVING

*130 calories, 2 gm. fat, 1 gm. saturated fat,
107 mg. cholesterol with egg (0 with egg sub.), 53 mg. sodium,
23 gm. carbohydrate, 4 gm. protein*

Count as 1 1/2 fruit and 1/2 lean meat for food exchange eating plans.

15 minutes "hands-on" preparation time, 30 minutes baking time

VALENTINE'S DAY

Significant Symbols

HEARTS

One story of Valentine origin takes place on February 14, 269 A.D. St. Valentine was in prison, and while there, he fell in love with the jailer's daughter. The love letters he signed, "From your Valentine" led Emperor Claudius to order his death. As time passed, this day became a time for exchanging love messages, and St. Valentine emerged as the patron saint of lovers.

ADD FUN, SUBTRACT EXPENSE

◆ *Use a cookie cutter to make heart-shaped toast for break-fast.*

◆ *Remember those who may not receive many valentine greetings.*

◆ *Make homemade valentines using red construction paper and white paper doilies, and exchange them at dinnertime. For fun, hide little love messages around the house, and let family members search for them.*

◆ *Instead of buying candy, relieve your family members of routine chores with coupons for "One take out the garbage" or "One complete car wash, inside and out."*

◆ Have a party and practice simple love songs. Then travel around the neighborhood, delivering your "singing valentines."

MENU IDEAS

LIGHT THE CANDLES DINNER

Sparkling Wine

Skinny Caesar Salad

Apricot Stuffed Pork Chops

Lemony California Blend Vegetables

Cherry Cheese Pie

ENJOY DINNER OUT AND COME HOME FOR

Cherry Chocolate Pie or
Sweetheart Cookies or
Meringue Shell with Strawberry Custard

SKINNY CAESAR SALAD

Serves 8, 2 cups each

DRESSING:

1 tube anchovy paste
1/2 tsp. minced garlic
2 Tbsp. lemon juice
2 Tbsp. Dijon mustard

3 Tbsp. olive oil
1/4 tsp. salt
1/2 tsp. pepper

SALAD:

1 large head romaine lettuce, chilled
1 basket cherry tomatoes, chilled

1/4 cup chopped black olives
1/2 cup grated Parmesan cheese
1 cup reduced-fat croutons

DRESSING: Combine first four ingredients in a small mixing bowl. Gradually mix in the oil. Add salt and pepper.

SALAD: Halve the cherry tomatoes. Tear lettuce leaves into bite-size pieces in a large salad bowl. Add tomatoes, olives, and cheese, tossing lightly. Add dressing mixture, and toss to coat all the leaves. Top with croutons and serve immediately on chilled plates.

NUTRIENTS PER SERVING

124 calories, 8 gm. fat, 1 gm. saturated fat, 3 mg. cholesterol, 393 mg. sodium, 8 gm. carbohydrate, 5 gm. protein

Count as 2 vegetable and 1 1/2 fat for food exchange eating plans.

15 minutes "hands-on" preparation time

APRICOT STUFFED PORK CHOPS

Serves 8

STUFFING:

4 oz. dried apricots, diced

1/4 cup brandy or red wine

1/3 cup hot water

1 small onion, chopped

2 Tbsp. melted margarine

2 tsp. fennel seed

1/2 tsp. white pepper

1/2 tsp. nutmeg

2 tsp. finely grated orange peel

2 eggs or 1/2 cup liquid egg substitute

8 oz. croutons

CHOPS:

Chicken broth

8 4-oz. pork chops

1/4 cup apricot preserves

1/4 cup chicken broth

Soak diced dried apricots in the brandy for at least 10 minutes or up to 24 hours. In a large mixing bowl, combine marinated apricots with all remaining ingredients. If mixture seems dry, add chicken broth to obtain appropriate consistency for stuffing.

Preheat oven to 350° F. Trim chops well. Make a pocket in the meat by slicing horizontally toward the bone halfway up the thickness of the chop. Stuff each chop with 1/3 cup of the prepared stuffing mixture. Spoon remaining stuffing into a baking dish that has been sprayed with nonstick cooking spray. In a 9- by 13-inch baking dish, combine apricot preserves and chicken broth. Spread evenly over bottom of the dish, then place stuffed chops on top. Cover with foil and bake for 20 minutes. Remove foil and bake for 20 more minutes. Chops will be brown on top. Pork is done when it reaches 160 degrees internally.

319 calories, 15 gm. fat, 5 gm. saturated fat, 161 mg. cholesterol with egg (108 mg. with egg sub.), 208 mg. sodium, 18 gm. carbohydrate, 28 gm. protein

Count as 1/2 fruit, 1 bread/starch, and 4 lean meat for food exchange eating plans.

20 minutes "hands-on" preparation time, 40 minutes baking time

LEMONY CALIFORNIA BLEND VEGETABLES

ONLY 1 GRAM OF FAT

Serves 8, 1/2 cup each

16-oz. frozen California blend vegetables

1 Tbsp. reduced-fat margarine

1 Tbsp. lemon juice

1 tsp. finely grated lemon rind

1/2 tsp. white pepper

Place frozen vegetables in an 11- by 7-inch baking dish. cover with plastic wrap and microwave on high power for 4 minutes. Meanwhile, combine margarine with lemon juice, lemon rind, and white pepper in a small bowl. Microwave the mixture for 30 seconds or just until the margarine is melted. Toss lemon juice mixture with steamed vegetables, and serve immediately.

NUTRIENTS PER SERVING

46 calories, 1 gm. fat, 0 saturated fat, 0 cholesterol, 36 mg. sodium, 7 gm. carbohydrate, 1 gm. protein

Count as 2 vegetable for food exchange eating plans.

10 minutes "hands-on" preparation time, 5 minutes cooking time

CHERRY CHEESE PIE

Serves 12

8-oz. carton nonfat lemon yogurt

8 oz. nonfat cream cheese, softened to room temperature

1 envelope unflavored gelatin

1/4 cup very cold water

1/2 cup white grape juice concentrate

1 prepared graham cracker crust

21-oz. can cherry pie filling

Combine yogurt and cream cheese in a large mixer bowl. Beat until blended and smooth. Set aside. In a small saucepan, sprinkle gelatin over cold water. Allow gelatin to soften for 1 minute, then cook over low heat, stirring constantly until gelatin is dissolved. Remove from heat, then stir in grape juice concentrate and yogurt mixture, beating well. Pour into prepared crust, then cover and refrigerate for at least 1 hour or up to overnight. Top with chilled cherry pie filling just before service.

NUTRIENTS PER SERVING

243 calories, 6 gm. fat, 1 gm. saturated fat, 1 mg. cholesterol, 184 mg. sodium, 44 gm. carbohydrate, 5 gm. protein

Count as 2 bread/starch, 1 fruit, and 1/2 fat for food exchange eating plans.

20 minutes "hands-on" preparation time, 60 minutes chilling time

CHERRY CHOCOLATE PIE

Serves 12

3-oz. package instant vanilla
 pudding mix

3-oz. package sugar-free cherry
 gelatin

1 1/2 cups skim milk

21-oz. can cherry pie filling

1 cup reduced-fat whipped
 topping

9-inch prepared chocolate
 flavored cookie crumb pie crust

OPTIONAL GARNISH: shaved
 chocolate

In a large bowl, combine dry pudding mix, dry gelatin, and skim milk. Use a wire whisk to blend. Stir in pie filling and whipped topping. Spread into the pie crust. Refrigerate for at least 30 minutes. If desired, garnish with shaved chocolate at serving time.

NUTRIENTS PER SERVING

*221 calories, 9 gm. fat, 3 gm. saturated fat, 1 mg. cholesterol,
160 mg. sodium, 34 gm. carbohydrate, 3 gm. protein*

Count as 2 bread/starch, 1/2 fruit, and 1 fat for food exchange eating plans.

15 minutes "hands-on" preparation time, 30 minutes chilling time

SWEETHEART COOKIES

FAT-FREE!

Serves 16, 1 cookie each

3 egg whites

1/4 tsp. cream of tartar

1/8 tsp. salt

6 drops red food coloring

1 tsp. almond extract

1/2 cup sugar

1/4 cup mini chocolate chips

Preheat oven to 225° F. In a medium mixing bowl, beat egg whites on high with an electric mixer until soft peaks form. Add cream of tartar, salt, food coloring, and almond extract. Continue beating and add sugar until stiff peaks form. Fold in chocolate chips. Drop meringue by spoonfuls to form 16 cookies. Bake for 45 minutes, then turn off the oven and let cookies dry in the oven for 1 hour. Remove from oven and store in a tightly covered container.

NUTRIENTS PER SERVING

40 calories, 0 fat, 0 saturated fat, 0 cholesterol, 27 mg. sodium, 7 gm. carbohydrate, 0 protein

Count as 1/2 fruit for food exchange eating plans.

15 minutes "hands-on" preparation time, 1 hour and 45 minutes baking time

MERINGUE SHELL WITH STRAWBERRY CUSTARD

ONLY 1 GRAM OF FAT

A super sweet Valentine dessert.
Serves 12

10 egg whites	1/2 tsp. vanilla
1/2 tsp. cream of tartar	1 cup sugar

Preheat oven to 350° F. Place oven rack in lowest position. Beat egg whites with an electric mixer on high until frothy. Add cream of tartar and vanilla. Gradually beat in sugar, a couple of spoonfuls at a time until meringue is stiff and shiny. With a spatula, pack meringue into a Bundt pan sprayed with nonstick cooking spray. Smooth out the meringue. Spray a sheet of foil with nonstick cooking spray and place it over the Bundt pan, sprayed side down.

Place the pan in a shallow baking dish and pour hot tap water into the dish, about 2 inches deep. Bake for 15 minutes. Remove mold from the water bath to a wire rack and let cool completely. Unmold the meringue onto a large round platter, slice into 12 servings, and spoon Strawberry Custard sauce all around it. To serve, place a serving of meringue on a dessert plate and top with several spoonsful of custard sauce.

STRAWBERRY CUSTARD SAUCE:

2 6-oz. cartons custard style strawberry yogurt

1 cup reduced-fat whipped topping

1 cup sliced fresh strawberries

Fold ingredients together in a mixing bowl, and serve with meringue.

NUTRIENTS PER SERVING

123 calories, 1 gm. fat, 0 saturated fat, 3 mg. cholesterol, 65 mg. sodium, 23 gm. carbohydrate, 4 gm. protein

Count as 2 fruit for food exchange eating plans.

20 minutes "hands-on" preparation time, 15 minutes baking time, 15 minutes cooling time

PRESIDENT'S DAY

Significant Symbols

GEORGE WASHINGTON

Washington was our nation's first president. Following the British custom to celebrate the king's birthday each year, the observance of Washington's birthday began following the American Revolution. Each year, patriotic programs in schools keep his memory alive, and we recall our forefathers with thanksgiving.

ABRAHAM LINCOLN

Born on February 12, President Abraham Lincoln abolished slavery and led the country through the Civil War period. Beginning in 1891, states began celebrating Lincoln's birthday as a legal holiday. Today he is honored together with Washington on President's Day, the third Monday of February.

ADD FUN, SUBTRACT EXPENSE

- ◆ *Observe after-dinner customs from Mount Vernon culture, such as card playing or ballroom dancing.*

- ◆ *Decorate the dinner table with American flags or a red, white, and blue tablecloth.*

- ◆ *If you have old coin books on the shelf, get them out, and look over your Washington quarters and Lincoln dimes.*

MENU IDEAS

George Washington Beefsteak Pie or
Mary Lincoln's Chicken Fricassee

Baked New Potatoes with Parsley

Mount Vernon Trifle or
Tell the Truth Cherry Parfait

GEORGE WASHINGTON BEEFSTEAK PIE

Serves 6

2 strips bacon, diced

1/2 lb. sirloin steak, cut into 1-inch pieces

1/4 cup flour

1 cup red wine

2 small onions, diced

2 bay leaves

1/2 cup chopped parsley

1/2 cup chopped celery, including leafy tops

1 cup sliced mushrooms

1/4 tsp. salt

1 tsp. black pepper

1 tsp. marjoram

1 1/2 cups reduced-fat baking mix, such as Bisquick® Light

1/2 cup beef broth

Preheat oven to 375° F. In a large skillet, cook bacon until crisp. Roll chunks of sirloin steak in flour, then add to bacon and sauté for 3 minutes, until well browned. Add wine, onions, bay leaves, parsley, celery, mushrooms, salt, pepper, and marjoram. Cover and simmer mixture for 10 minutes. Meanwhile, spray an 11- by 7-inch baking dish with nonstick cooking spray. Use a fork to combine baking mix and beef broth in a small bowl. Mix just until liquid is absorbed; dough will be sticky. Pour beef and vegetable mixture into prepared baking pan. Use a spoon to dollop biscuit dough on top of beef and vegetable mixture. Bake for 20 minutes until biscuits are golden brown.

NUTRIENTS PER SERVING

*306 calories, 8 gm. fat, 2 gm. saturated fat, 32 mg. cholesterol,
825 mg. sodium (to reduce sodium, use no-added-salt beef broth, and omit salt),
42 gm. carbohydrate, 17 gm. protein*

*Count as 2 bread/starch, 2 lean meat, and 2 vegetable for
food exchange eating plans.*

20 minutes "hands-on" preparation time, 35 minutes total cooking time

MARY LINCOLN'S CHICKEN FRICASSEE
ONLY 3 GRAMS OF FAT

Serves 4

2 whole chicken breasts, skinned,
  boned, and halved

1/4 tsp. salt

1/4 tsp. pepper

1/4 tsp. nutmeg

1/4 tsp. mace

1/4 tsp. marjoram

1 cup evaporated skim milk

OPTIONAL GARNISH: fresh
  parsley

Season chicken with salt, pepper, nutmeg, mace and marjoram. Place in a large skillet. Pour milk over chicken. Cook over medium-low heat for 20 minutes, until chicken is tender. Garnish with fresh parsley.

NUTRIENTS PER SERVING

*186 calories, 3 gm. fat, 0 saturated fat, 74 mg. cholesterol,
261 mg. sodium, 6 gm. carbohydrate, 30 gm. protein*

Count as 3 1/2 lean meat for food exchange eating plans.

10 minutes "hands-on" preparation time, 20 minutes cooking time

BAKED NEW POTATOES WITH PARSLEY

ONLY 3 GRAMS OF FAT

Serves 4, 2 small potatoes each

8 small new potatoes, scrubbed
    clean
1/4 tsp. salt

1 Tbsp. vegetable oil
1/4 cup minced fresh parsley

Preheat oven to 400° F. In a large bowl, mix potatoes with salt, oil, and parsley. Turn out onto a metal pie pan to bake. Bake for 45 to 50 minutes, or until potatoes test tender with a fork.

NUTRIENTS PER SERVING

*195 calories, 3 gm. fat, 0 saturated fat, 0 cholesterol,
145 mg. sodium, 38 gm. carbohydrate, 4 gm. protein*

Count as 2 bread/starch and 1/2 fat for food exchange eating plans.

10 minutes "hands-on" preparation time, 50 minutes baking time

MOUNT VERNON TRIFLE

ONLY 2 GRAMS OF FAT

Serves 16

CUSTARD LAYER:
3 cups skim milk
1/2 cup sugar
6 whole eggs or 1 1/2 cups liquid
    egg substitute

1 cup skim milk
1 tsp. almond extract

In a medium saucepan, combine 3 cups skim milk with sugar. Heat to scalding. Meanwhile, in a medium mixing bowl, beat eggs with

1 cup skim milk. Gradually add the egg mixture to the scalded milk. Stir continuously over medium-low heat until the custard coats a spoon. Stir in almond extract. Chill.

Meanwhile, assemble fruit and cake layers:

FRUIT AND CAKE LAYER:

1 prepared sponge cake (such as Sara Lee® light), cut into 1-inch chunks

1/2 cup sweet white wine

1 cup mixed dried fruits, such as dates, raisins, pineapple, apricot, apple, pear, or papaya

Place chunks of sponge cake in a clear glass trifle dish or deep serving bowl. Sprinkle with white wine and 3/4 cup dried fruits. When custard is cooled to room temperature, spoon over cake and fruit. Decorate the top with reserved 1/4 cup dried fruit. Refrigerate until service.

NUTRIENTS PER SERVING

193 calories, 2 gm. fat, 1 gm. saturated fat, 110 mg. cholesterol with egg (30 mg. with egg sub.), 127 mg. sodium, 34 gm. carbohydrate, 6 gm. protein

Count as 1 bread/starch, 1 1/2 fruit, and 1/2 fat for food exchange eating plans.

20 minutes "hands-on" preparation time

TELL THE TRUTH CHERRY PARFAIT

ONLY 1 GRAM OF FAT

Serves 8

1 cup fat-free ricotta cheese	2 Tbsp. very hot tap water
1/2 cup powdered sugar	21-oz. can cherry pie filling
1/2 cup nonfat sour cream	16 reduced-fat white sandwich
1 Tbsp. instant coffee	cookies (such as Snackwells®)

In a mixing bowl, combine cheese with sugar and sour cream. In a small bowl, stir coffee into water. Fold dissolved coffee into ricotta mixture and set aside. Remove 8 cherries from the the pie filling and reserve for garnish. Place the cookies in a heavy plastic bag and crush with a rolling pin.

To assemble parfaits, layer cherry pie filling, cookie crumbs and cheese twice into 8 parfait glasses. Finish with reserved cherry. Chill until service.

NUTRIENTS PER SERVING

186 calories, 1 gm. fat, 0 saturated fat, 3 mg. cholesterol, 66 mg. sodium, 40 gm. carbohydrate, 6 gm. protein

Count as 2 bread/starch and 1/2 fruit for food exchange eating plans.

20 minutes "hands-on" preparation time

Significant Symbols

SHAMROCKS

St. Patrick first used the three-leaved shamrock to represent the trinity of the Father, Son, and Holy Spirit. St. Patrick was a priest and later a bishop who was sent to Ireland to convert the Druids to Christianity. We celebrate his memory on March 17, the day of his death in 493 A.D.

GREEN

The color of shamrocks, Ireland's chief emblem, and the color of the Emerald Isle itself, green is worn by people of Irish origin all around the world who celebrate the holiday.

ADD FUN, SUBTRACT EXPENSE

- ◆ *Check out some Irish music from your library, or sit down at the piano and pound out "When Irish Eyes are Smiling," or "The Wearin' of the Green," or "My Wild Irish Rose."*

- ◆ *Plan to attend a St. Patrick's Day parade near you.*

- ◆ *Remember St. Patrick's bravery and commitment to good in a table blessing.*

- ◆ *Decorate your table with green placemats or candles. Splurge on some green tinted carnations for the centerpiece.*

MENU IDEAS

EAT, DRINK, AND BE MERRY LUNCHEON

Frosty Lime Fizz

Reuben Dip or
Hot Broccoli Dip with Sour Dough Dippers

Leek and Potato Soup

Raisin Scones

Fruited Coleslaw

Irish Cappuccino

WEAR SOMETHING GREEN TO DINNER

Corned Beef and Cabbage

Potato Bread in the Machine

Pickled Beets

Frozen Fruit Creme

Perfect Green Tea

FROSTY LIME FIZZ

FAT-FREE!

Serves 8, 10 oz. each

6 oz. frozen pineapple juice
  concentrate

1 1/2 cups water

1/4 cup lime juice

2 cups lime sherbet

32 oz. sugar-free lemon lime
  soft drink

Put pineapple juice concentrate, water, lime juice, and 1 cup of sherbet into a blender container. Blend until smooth. Pour mixture into 8 10-12 oz. glasses. Add remaining lime sherbet to each glass. Fill each glass to the top with soft drink.

NUTRIENTS PER SERVING

*117 calories, 0 fat, 0 saturated fat, 3 mg. cholesterol,
16 mg. sodium, 27 gm. carbohydrate, 0 protein*

Count as 2 fruit for food exchange eating plans.

15 minutes "hands-on" preparation time

REUBEN DIP

Serves 8, 1/3 cup each

8-oz. package reduced-fat
  cream cheese, softened to
  room temperature

1/2 cup nonfat sour cream

3 oz. reduced-fat Swiss cheese,
  shredded

2 2 1/2-oz. packages corned beef,
  cut in pieces

1/2 cup sauerkraut, drained well

1/4 tsp. white pepper

1/8 tsp. garlic powder

Mix all ingredients together and chill. Serve with Rye Crisps®.

NUTRIENTS PER SERVING

*107 calories, 4 gm. fat, 1 gm. saturated fat, 15 mg. cholesterol,
129 mg. sodium, 2 gm. carbohydrate, 11 gm. protein*

Count as 1 lean meat and 1 fat for food exchange eating plans.

10 minutes "hands-on" preparation time

HOT BROCCOLI DIP WITH SOURDOUGH DIPPERS

Serves 12

1 1/2 lb. round sourdough bread loaf

2 ribs celery, finely chopped

1 medium red pepper, finely chopped

1 green onion, finely chopped

1 Tbsp. reduced-fat margarine

8 oz. reduced-fat pasteurized processed cheese (such as Velveeta® light)

10-oz. pkg. frozen chopped broccoli, thawed and drained

1/2 tsp. dried rosemary

Preheat oven to 350° F. Cut the top off the bread loaf. Remove the bread from the center, leaving a 1-inch shell. Cut removed bread into bite-size pieces. Place top back on shell, and place loaf on a cookie sheet with bread cubes around it. Bake for 15 minutes, until hot. Meanwhile, in a skillet, sauté celery, peppers, and onions in margarine. Add cubed cheese and stir until melted. Stir in remaining ingredients, and heat until bubbly. Spoon broccoli mixture into the bread shell and serve with bread cubes.

NUTRIENTS PER SERVING

*103 calories, 4 gm. fat, 2 gm. saturated fat, 10 mg. cholesterol,
415 mg. sodium, 11 gm. carbohydrate, 6 gm. protein*

Count as 1/2 bread/starch, 1 vegetable, and 1 fat for food exchange eating plans.

15 minutes "hands-on" preparation time, 15 minutes baking time

LEEK AND POTATO SOUP

ONLY 2 GRAMS OF FAT

*My friend Mary Sadewasser discovered this wonderful recipe for leeks.
Serves 8, 1 1/2 cups each*

4 cups chicken broth

4 large potatoes, peeled and diced

1 large leek, chopped

1 grated carrot

1 Tbsp. dried parsley

1 1/2 cups evaporated skim milk

1 1/2 cups skim milk

1 cup cooked diced chicken

1/2 tsp. white pepper

1/4 tsp. salt

OPTIONAL GARNISH:
carrot curls

In a large pan, bring broth to simmering. Add potatoes, leeks, and carrots. Cover and simmer for 20 minutes. Partially mash potatoes in broth. Add parsley and milks. Add chicken, pepper, and salt, and continue to cook for 5 minutes. Garnish bowls of soup with carrot curls.

NUTRIENTS PER SERVING

*177 calories, 2 gm. fat, 0 saturated fat, 26 mg. cholesterol,
827 mg. sodium (to reduce sodium, use no-salt-added chicken broth),
21 gm. carbohydrate, 15 gm. protein*

Count as 1 bread/starch and 1 skim milk for food exchange eating plans.

15 minutes "hands-on" preparation time, 30 minutes cooking time

RAISIN SCONES
ONLY 3 GRAMS OF FAT

Serves 12, 1 scone each

2 cups flour

1 1/2 tsp. baking power

3/4 tsp. salt

3 Tbsp. sugar

1 1/2 tsp. caraway seed

2 Tbsp. vegetable oil

1 cup low-fat buttermilk

2/3 cup chopped raisins

2 Tbsp. sugar

Preheat oven to 350° F. In a large bowl, mix flour with other dry ingredients. Stir in caraway seeds. Make a well in the center of the mixture. Pour in the oil and buttermilk. Add raisins and mix lightly to make a soft dough. Turn the dough out onto a floured board, and knead gently for a few strokes. Shape the dough into a round shape, and place it in a 9-inch round layer cake pan that has been sprayed with nonstick cooking spray. Cut loaf crosswise into quarters about two-thirds through the dough, using a sharp knife or scissors. Sprinkle sugar on top of the dough. Bake for 30 minutes.

NUTRIENTS PER SERVING

205 calories, 3 gm. fat, 0 saturated fat, 1 mg. cholesterol, 201 mg. sodium, 47 gm. carbohydrate, 6 gm. protein

Count as 2 bread/starch and 1 fat for food exchange eating plans.

15 minutes "hands-on" preparation time, 30 minutes baking time

FRUITED COLESLAW
ONLY 3 GRAMS OF FAT

Serves 8, 1 cup each

1-lb. bag shredded cabbage

1 medium Delicious apple, cored and diced

8-oz. can pineapple tidbits in juice, drained well

1/2 cup green grapes, halved

DRESSING:

2 Tbsp. vegetable oil

1/4 cup lime juice

1 Tbsp. vinegar

1/4 cup sugar

Combine cabbage with diced apple, pineapple tidbits, and grape halves in a salad bowl. In a shaker container, combine ingredients for dressing. Pour over vegetables and fruit, and toss to coat.

NUTRIENTS PER SERVING

118 calories, 3 gm. fat, 0 saturated fat, 0 cholesterol, 10 mg. sodium, 21 gm. carbohydrate, 1 gm. protein

Count as 1 fruit, 1 vegetable, and 1/2 fat for food exchange eating plans.

15 minutes "hands-on" preparation time

IRISH CAPPUCCINO
FAT-FREE!

Serves 8

4 oz. chocolate syrup

4 oz. Irish cream syrup or Bailey's Irish Cream® liqueur

5 oz. espresso

2 cups steamed skim milk foam from espresso machine

Dash of cocoa

Pour syrups and espresso into 8 demitasse (small coffee cups). Top with foam and dash of cocoa.

NUTRIENTS PER SERVING (ANALYSIS WITH IRISH CREAM LIQUEUR)

127 calories, 0 fat, 0 saturated fat, 2 mg. cholesterol, 30 mg. sodium, 10 gm. carbohydrate, 2 gm. protein

Count as 1 skim milk and 1/2 fruit for food exchange eating plans.

15 minutes "hands-on" preparation time

CORNED BEEF AND CABBAGE

Serves 8

2 lb. corned brisket of beef, wiped with damp paper toweling

2 quarts cold water

6 peppercorns

6 whole allspice

1 bay leaf

1 large yellow onion, peeled and quartered

1 large cabbage, trimmed of coarse leaves, cored, and cut into 8 wedges

OPTIONAL GARNISH: horseradish sauce

Place brisket into a large kettle. Fill with water, add peppercorns, allspice, bay leaf, and onion. Cover and bring to a boil over high heat. Reduce heat to low and simmer for 10 minutes. Skim off top layer of fat. Recover and simmer for 3 hours or until tender. Again, skim off any fat from the cooking water. Add cabbage during last 15 minutes of cooking. Arrange cabbage wedges around the outside of a large platter. Carve corned beef against the grain in thin slices. Garnish slices with horseradish sauce.

••

NUTRIENTS PER SERVING

*209 calories, 9 gm. fat, 5.8 gm. saturated fat, 173 mg. cholesterol,
122 mg. sodium, 4 gm. carbohydrate, 26 gm. protein*

Count as 3 lean meat and 2 vegetable for food exchange eating plans.

10 minutes "hands-on" preparation time, 3 1/2 hours cooking time

POTATO BREAD IN THE MACHINE

ONLY 2 GRAMS OF FAT

Serves 12, 1 slice each

7/8 cup water	1 1/2 Tbsp. sugar
1/3 cup mashed potatoes	1 tsp. salt
3 cups white bread flour	1 1/2 tsp. active dry yeast
2 Tbsp. nonfat dry milk	1 Tbsp. soft margarine

This recipe has been tested with a Hitachi Home Bakery®. Add ingredients in order listed to the bread pan. Push start. Bread is done in 4 hours and 10 minutes.

NUTRIENTS PER SERVING

*149 calories, 2 gm. fat, 0 saturated fat, 1 mg. cholesterol,
36 mg. sodium, 28 gm. carbohydrate, 5 gm. protein*

Count as 2 bread/starch for food exchange eating plans.

10 minutes "hands-on" preparation time, 4 hours and 10 minutes baking time

PICKLED BEETS

FAT-FREE!

Serves 8, 1/2 cup each

2 bunches fresh beets	2 Tbsp. sugar
Boiling salted water	1/8 tsp. ground cloves
1 medium onion, sliced thin	1/2 tsp. salt
1/2 cup vinegar	3 peppercorns
1/2 cup water	1/2 bay leaf

Wash beets, leaving root intact. Cut off all but 2 inches of tops. Add beets to the boiling water and cook for 20 minutes, or until tender. Remove from water, cool and peel. Slice or quarter the beets into a salad bowl that can be covered. Sprinkle sliced onion over beets. In a small saucepan, combine all remaining ingredients and bring to a boil. Pour the mixture over the beets, cover and refrigerate for at least 48 hours before serving.

NUTRIENTS PER SERVING

59 calories, 0 fat, 0 saturated fat, 0 cholesterol, 199 mg. sodium, 14 gm. carbohydrate, 2 gm. protein

Count as 2 vegetables for food exchange eating plans.

15 minutes "hands-on" preparation time, 20 minutes cooking time, 48 hours chilling time

● ●

FROZEN FRUIT CREAM

ONLY 3 GRAMS OF FAT

Serves 12

11-oz. can mandarin oranges, well drained

8-oz. can crushed pineapple, well drained

1 Tbsp. finely grated orange rind

1 Tbsp. marsala or sweet wine

3 cups nonfat vanilla frozen yogurt

1 cup reduced-fat whipped topping

Drain oranges and pineapple well. Fold drained fruit, orange rind, and marsala into the frozen yogurt. Fold in whipped topping. Turn into a high sided quiche dish and freeze for at least 3 hours. Cut into 12 wedges and serve with reduced-fat shortbread cookies (such as Snackwells®) and green tea.

NUTRIENTS PER SERVING

148 calories, 3 gm. fat, 2 gm. saturated fat, 0 cholesterol, 36 mg. sodium, 29 gm. carbohydrate, 2 gm. protein

Count as 2 fruit and 1/2 fat for food exchange eating plans.

15 minutes "hands-on" preparation time, 3 hours chilling time

PERFECT GREEN TEA

FAT-FREE!

This recipe is in memory of all my Grandmother McCracken's family, who taught me to drink green tea when I was but a "wee bit of a girl."

Loose green tea   Cold tap water

Scald a china, heatproof glass, or porcelain teapot with boiling water. (Don't use a metal teapot.) For each serving, use 3/4 cup water and 1 tsp. loose green tea. Place required quantity of cold water in a teakettle, and bring to a full boil. Meanwhile, place tea in the scalded teapot, pour boiling water directly over the tea, and allow to steep for 5 minutes. Serve from the teapot over a small strainer into china teacups. Add milk, sugar, or lemon juice if desired.

NUTRIENTS PER SERVING

0 calories, 0 fat, 0 saturated fat, 0 cholesterol, 0 sodium, 0 carbohydrate, 0 protein

Count as a free food for food exchange eating plans.

10 minutes "hands-on" preparation time

EASTER SEASON

Significant Symbols

FASTING AND REPENTANCE

Lent is the period of 40 days, excluding Sundays, that begins with Ash Wednesday and ends the day before Easter. The traditional observance of fasting, self-denial, and devotion is to commemorate Christ's 40 days in the wilderness and prepare for Easter.

PALMS

Palm Sunday, the Sunday before Easter, is the first day of Holy Week. The name came from the custom of carrying palm branches on feast days in observance of Christ's triumphal entry into Jerusalem. The palm has been a symbol of elegance and grace for centuries.

EASTER RABBIT AND EGGS

The idea that the Easter rabbit laid eggs for children to search for in the grass came from Germany. This custom originated from the fact that rabbits are prolific and hence a symbol of fertility. In medieval Europe, poultry eggs were scarce and the gift of an egg was gratefully received. Colored Easter eggs go as far back as early Egyptians, who dyed eggs for spring festivals. The bright colors symbolize the arrival of spring. Egg-rolling is said to have come from the idea of rolling away the stone from Christ's tomb. The custom of rolling hard-boiled eggs down a hill was brought to the new world by British settlers and is still continued at the White House today.

ADD FUN, SUBTRACT EXPENSE

◆ *Shrove Tuesday or Fat Tuesday is the day before Ash Wednesday. Celebrate the day known for using up the last bit of fat before Lent with a pancake supper.*

◆ *Try meatless recipes during the Lenten season.*

◆ *During Holy Week, look at art inspired by the life of Jesus either in a museum or in an art book from the library.*

◆ *Put candles in your windows during Holy Week.*

◆ *Consider a simple menu on Maundy Thursday of unleavened bread, grape juice, eggs, cinnamon apples, and nuts.*

◆ *Make hot cross buns on Good Friday. Save time by using refrigerated cinnamon rolls and shaping the frosting in the form of a cross.*

◆ *Make quick and simple Easter baskets using wood or plastic mesh berry baskets from the grocery store.*

◆ *Surprise your kids by using their favorite cereal bowl for an Easter basket, and have it on the table when they get up.*

◆ *Give the kids a kite, and spend Easter Sunday flying it.*

◆ *Celebrate the new life of spring by preparing for the garden. Plant some seeds on Easter afternoon.*

....

MENU IDEAS

ASH WEDNESDAY

Saucy Tuna Casserole

Honey of a Grapefruit Salad

Low-Fat Carrot Cake

MEATLESS FRIDAY ENTREES

Hot Seafood Salad or Crabmeat Cakes

FIRST DAY OF PASSOVER OR PALM SUNDAY DINNER

Orange Glazed Cornish Hens

Potato Balls

Gingered Asparagus

Apricot Loaf

EASTER SUNDAY DINNER

Baked Ham with Apples

Mashed Potatoes with Low-Fat Holiday Gravy

Sugared Carrots

Horseradish Coleslaw

Sour Cream Lemon Meringue Pie

Traditional Lemon Meringue Pie with No Weep Meringue

SAUCY TUNA CASSEROLE

Serves 8, 1 1/2 cups each

2 6-oz. cans chunk tuna in water, well drained

2 10-oz. cans reduced fat cream of mushroom soup

16 oz. frozen broccoli

1/2 tsp. dill weed

2 cups reduced-fat baking mix, such as Bisquick® light

1 1/2 cups skim milk

1 tsp. parsley flakes

Preheat oven to 450° F. Mix tuna, soup, broccoli, and dill weed in an ungreased 13- by 9-inch baking dish. Stir baking mix and milk together in a small bowl until blended. Pour over tuna, and sprinkle with parsley. Bake for 30 minutes or until crust is light brown.

NUTRIENTS PER SERVING

*306 calories, 5 gm. fat, 0 saturated fat, 13 mg. cholesterol,
1015 mg. sodium (to reduce sodium, use low-sodium tuna),
44 gm. carbohydrate, 15 gm. protein*

*Count as 2 bread/starch, 2 lean meat, and 1 vegetable
for food exchange eating plans.*

15 minutes "hands-on" preparation time, 30 minutes baking time

HONEY OF A GRAPEFRUIT SALAD

FAT-FREE!

Serves 4, 3/4 cup each

14-oz. can grapefruit sections, drained

11-oz. can mandarin oranges, drained

2 Tbsp. lemon juice

2 Tbsp. honey

1/4 tsp. cinnamon

Combine drained fruits in a salad bowl. Sprinkle with lemon juice, drizzle with honey, sprinkle with cinnamon and toss. Serve at room temperature or chilled.

NUTRIENTS PER SERVING

*134 calories, 0 fat, 0 saturated fat, 0 cholesterol, 2 mg. sodium,
34 gm. carbohydrate, 1 gm. protein*

Count as 2 fruit for food exchange eating plans.

10 minutes "hands-on" preparation time

LOW-FAT CARROT CAKE

ONLY 2 GRAMS OF FAT

Serves 24

1 94% fat-free yellow cake mix

1 1/4 cups nonfat mayonnaise or salad dressing

4 eggs or 1 cup liquid egg substitute

1/4 cup cold water

2 tsp. ground cinnamon

2 cups finely shredded carrots

2 Tbsp. chopped walnuts

Preheat oven to 350° F. In a large bowl, combine cake mix, mayonnaise, eggs, water, and cinnamon with an electric mixer. Blend on medium speed for 2 minutes. Fold in carrots and pour into a 13-by 9-inch cake pan that has been sprayed with nonstick cooking spray. Sprinkle chopped walnuts over the cake batter, and bake for 35 minutes or until a toothpick inserted in the center comes out clean. Cut into 24 servings. If desired, serve with nonfat frozen vanilla yogurt.

NUTRIENTS PER SERVING

118 calories, 2 gm. fat, 0 saturated fat, 29 mg. cholesterol with egg (0 with egg sub.), 358 mg. sodium, 24 gm. carbohydrate, 2 gm. protein

Count as 1 bread/starch, 1 vegetable, and 1/2 fat for food exchange eating plans.

15 minutes "hands-on" preparation time, 35 minutes baking time

HOT SEAFOOD SALAD

ONLY 2 GRAMS OF FAT

Serves 8, 1 cup each

1 lb. crab or mock crab,
  flaked or diced fine

1 cup cooked shrimp

1 small onion, finely chopped

1 stalk celery, finely chopped

1/2 large green pepper, chopped

1 cup reduced-fat mayonnaise

1/4 tsp. seasoned salt

1 tsp. Worcestershire sauce

1/8 tsp. cracked pepper

1 cup plain croutons

1 Tbsp. soft margarine, melted

Preheat oven to 350° F. Combine crab and shrimp in a 2-quart casserole dish. Combine all remaining ingredients except croutons and margarine in a large bowl. Fold dressing into seafood. Toss croutons with melted margarine and sprinkle over casserole. Bake for 25 minutes.

NUTRIENTS PER SERVING

*132 calories, 2 gm. fat, 0 saturated fat, 57 mg. cholesterol,
1133 mg. sodium (to reduce sodium, omit salt and use fresh crab),
10 gm. carbohydrate, 15 gm. protein*

Count as 2 lean meat and 1/2 fat for food exchange eating plans.

15 minutes "hands-on" preparation time, 25 minutes baking time

CRABMEAT CAKES

ONLY 1 GRAM OF FAT

Serves 8, 1 pattie each

1/2 small green pepper, diced

1/4 cup fresh parsley, minced

2 green onions, diced

1 lb. crab or mock crab, flaked or diced fine

1 Tbsp. soft margarine

1/2 tsp. salt

1/4 tsp. cayenne pepper

1 egg white

1 Tbsp. reduced-fat mayonnaise

1 tsp. Worcestershire sauce

1 tsp. prepared mustard

1/2 cup bread crumbs

Preheat oven to 400° F. In a medium skillet, sauté pepper, parsley and green onions in margarine for 5 minutes. Add crab, salt, and cayenne. Remove from heat and cool. In a small mixing bowl, combine egg white, mayonnaise, Worcestershire sauce and mustard. Stir in bread crumbs, and mix with crab. Form into 8 patties. Place formed patties on a baking sheet sprayed with nonstick cooking spray, and bake for 30 minutes.

NUTRIENTS PER SERVING

96 calories, 1 gm. fat, 0 saturated fat, 11 mg. cholesterol, 758 mg. sodium (to reduce sodium, omit salt), 11 gm. carbohydrate, 7 gm. protein

Count as 1 lean meat and 1/2 bread/starch for food exchange eating plans.

15 minutes "hands-on" preparation time, 30 minutes baking time

ORANGE GLAZED CORNISH HENS

Serves 8

8 Rock Cornish hens, at least 1 lb. each

1 tsp. white pepper

1 cup all fruit orange preserves

1/2 cup reduced-sodium chicken stock

Preheat oven to 350° F. Clean hens and remove neck, heart, and gizzard. Discard innards, or use for making stock. Rub outside of hens with white pepper. Place hens, uncovered, on a rack over a roasting pan. Roast for 30 minutes. Then combine orange preserves with chicken stock in a small bowl. Spoon preserve mixture over hens at 15 minute intervals, until hens are fork tender, approximately 1 1/2 hours total baking time.

NUTRIENTS PER SERVING (NUTRITIONAL ANALYSIS BASED ON PERDUE® CORNISH HENS WITHOUT SKIN)
295 calories, 12 gm. fat, 4 gm. saturated fat, 214 mg. cholesterol, 69 mg. sodium, 10 gm. carbohydrate, 33 gm. protein

Count as 4 1/2 lean meat and 1 fruit for food exchange eating plans.

15 minutes "hands-on" preparation time, 1 hour and 30 minutes roasting time

POTATO BALLS

FAT-FREE!

Serves 8, 1/2 cup each

Instant mashed potato mix

3/4 cup nonfat sour cream

1 tsp. oregano

2 Tbsp. Parmesan cheese

1/3 cup bread crumbs

Preheat oven to 375° F. Prepare instant mashed potato mix as directed for 6 servings, substituting sour cream for the milk and butter. Stir in oregano and Parmesan cheese, then chill for 10 minutes. Shape potatoes into 8 balls, and coat with bread crumbs. Place on a baking sheet, and bake for 15 minutes.

NUTRIENTS PER SERVING

92 calories, 0 fat, 0 saturated fat, 0 cholesterol, 281 mg. sodium, 18 gm. carbohydrate, 4 gm. protein

Count as 1 bread/starch for food exchange eating plans.

15 minutes "hands-on" preparation time, 15 minutes baking time

GINGERED ASPARAGUS

ONLY 3 GRAMS OF FAT

Serves 8, 3/4 cup each

2 Tbsp. vegetable oil   2 tsp. ground ginger
2 lb. asparagus, trimmed and cut
   into 2-inch pieces

Heat oil until very hot in a large skillet over medium heat. Stir-fry asparagus and ginger for 8 minutes, or until tender crisp.

NUTRIENTS PER SERVING

55 calories, 3 gm. fat, 0 saturated fat, 0 cholesterol, 1 mg. sodium, 4 gm. carbohydrate, 3 gm. protein

Count as 1 vegetable and 1/2 fat for food exchange eating plans.

10 minutes "hands-on" preparation time, 10 minutes cooking time

APRICOT LOAF

ONLY 2 GRAMS OF FAT

Tammy Schmitt found this fruity favorite.
Serves 16, 1 slice each

3/4 cup dried apricots, minced

1/2 cup raisins, diced

1 cup boiling water

1 fresh orange

2/3 cup packed brown sugar

2 Tbsp. soft margarine, melted

1 egg or 1/4 cup liquid
  egg substitute

1 tsp. vanilla

2 cups flour

2 tsp. baking powder

1 tsp. salt

1 tsp. baking soda

Preheat oven to 350° F. In a large mixing bowl, allow apricots and raisins to stand in boiling water for 10 minutes. Using a vegetable peeler, remove zest from half of the orange, and add to fruit. Squeeze all of the juice from the orange and add to fruit mixture. Add brown sugar, margarine, egg, and vanilla to fruit, and blend well. In a separate bowl, combine dry ingredients. Fold into fruit just until all of the flour is moist. Turn into a loaf pan sprayed with nonstick cooking spray, and bake for 55 minutes or until bread tests done with a toothpick. This makes 1 large or 2 small loaves.

NUTRIENTS PER SERVING

178 calories, 2 gm. fat, 0 saturated fat, 13 mg. cholesterol with egg
(0 with egg sub.), 297 mg. sodium, 36 gm. carbohydrate, 4 gm. protein

Count as 1 bread/starch, 1 fruit, and 1/2 fat for food exchange eating plans.

20 minutes "hands-on" preparation time, 55 minutes baking time

BAKED HAM WITH APPLES

Serves 8, 3 oz. meat + 1/2 apple each

2 lb. 97% fat-free ham, cut into
8 slices

4 tart apples (such as Jonathan),
pared and sliced

1/3 cup flour

1/2 cup brown sugar

1 Tbsp. margarine, melted

Preheat oven to 350° F. Cut ham into serving portions and place on the bottom of a 9- by 13-inch baking dish that has been sprayed with nonstick cooking spray. Arrange the apple slices over the ham. In a small mixing bowl, mix the flour, brown sugar, and margarine together until crumbly, and sprinkle over the apples. Cover the pan and bake for 20 minutes. Remove the cover and bake for 10 more minutes or until apples are tender.

NUTRIENTS PER SERVING

295 calories, 7 gm. fat, 2 gm. saturated fat, 59 mg. cholesterol, 1385 mg. sodium (to reduce sodium, use reduced-sodium ham), 34 gm. carbohydrate, 24 gm. protein

Count as 3 lean meat and 2 fruit for food exchange eating plans.

15 minutes "hands-on" preparation time, 30 minutes baking time

LOW-FAT HOLIDAY GRAVY

ONLY 1 GRAM OF FAT

Serves 8, 1/4 cup each

2 cups no-added-salt chicken broth

1/4 cup flour

1 low sodium chicken bouillon
cube

1 tsp. browning sauce
(such as Kitchen Bouquet®)

1/8 tsp. white pepper

Blend 1/2 cup cold broth with flour in a small mixing bowl until smooth. Heat remaining broth with bouillon cube in a small saucepan. Stir flour mixture into the hot broth, and cook and stir over medium heat until mixture thickens. Reduce heat and add browning sauce and pepper. Serve over mashed potatoes.

NUTRIENTS PER SERVING

*38 calories, 1 gm. fat, 0 saturated fat, 0 cholesterol,
172 mg. sodium, 5 gm. carbohydrate, 1 gm. protein*

Count as 1/2 bread/starch for food exchange eating plans,

15 minutes "hands-on" preparation time

SUGARED CARROTS

ONLY 1 GRAM OF FAT

Serves 8, 1/2 cup each

2 lb. carrots
1/4 cup water
2 Tbsp. soft margarine

3 Tbsp. brown sugar
1/4 tsp. salt
1/8 tsp. white pepper

Cut each carrot crosswise in half; cut each half lengthwise into matchstick-thin strips. In a medium pan over high heat, combine carrots with water; cover and cook for 10 minutes. Drain. Add margarine, brown sugar, salt, and pepper to the carrots, continuing to heat until margarine and sugar are melted.

NUTRIENTS PER SERVING

81 calories, 1 gm. fat, 0 saturated fat, 0 cholesterol,
140 mg. sodium, 16 gm. carbohydrate, 1 gm. protein

Count as 1 vegetable and 1 fruit for food exchange eating plans.

15 minutes "hands-on" preparation time, 15 minutes cooking time

HORSERADISH COLESLAW

Serves 8, 1 cup each

1-lb. bag shredded cabbage and
  carrots
2 stalks celery, finely diced

4 green onions, diced
1 firm ripe tomato, seeded and
  chopped

DRESSING:

1/2 cup reduced-fat mayonnaise	2 Tbsp. sugar
1/4 tsp. lemon pepper	1 Tbsp. vinegar
1 Tbsp. prepared horseradish	1 tsp. celery seed

Combine vegetables in a large salad bowl. In a shaker container, mix ingredients for dressing. Pour dressing over salad, mix and refrigerate for up to an hour, or serve immediately. Omit the tomato if you want to refrigerate leftovers for the next day.

NUTRIENTS PER SERVING

104 calories, 6 gm. fat, 2 gm. saturated fat, 13 mg. cholesterol, 91 mg. sodium, 10 gm. carbohydrate, 4 gm. protein

Count as 2 vegetable and 1 fat for food exchange eating plans.

15 minutes "hands-on" preparation time

SOUR CREAM LEMON MERINGUE PIE

Serves 12

1 cup sugar
1/4 cup cornstarch
1/8 tsp. salt
1 cup skim milk
3 egg yolks, beaten
2 Tbsp. soft margarine

1/4 cup fresh-squeezed lemon juice
1 tsp. finely grated lemon peel
1 cup nonfat sour cream
1 prepared 9-inch graham cracker crust

MERINGUE:

3 egg whites
1/2 tsp. vanilla extract

1/4 tsp. cream of tartar
6 Tbsp. sugar

Preheat oven to 350° F. In a medium saucepan, combine sugar, cornstarch, and salt. Gradually stir in the milk. Bring mixture to a boil over medium heat, stirring constantly. Cook and stir for 2 minutes. Blend a small amount of the hot mixture into the egg yolks. Mix well, then put the egg mixture in the pan. Cook over medium heat, stirring constantly for 2 more minutes. Remove from the heat, and add margarine, lemon juice, and peel. Mix well and set aside. For meringue, beat egg whites until foamy. Add vanilla and cream of tartar. Add sugar, 1 tablespoon at a time, beating until stiff peaks form. Set aside. Fold sour cream into the lemon mixture, and pour into prepared crust. Cover the lemon with meringue, sealing edges to the crumbs. Bake for 12 minutes or until golden.

NUTRIENTS PER SERVING

219 calories, 6 gm. fat, 2 gm. saturated fat, 54 mg. cholesterol, 201 mg. sodium, 36 gm. carbohydrate, 4 gm. protein

Count as 1 1/2 fruit, 1 bread/starch, and 1 fat for food exchange eating plans.

20 minutes "hands-on" preparation time, 15 minutes baking time

TRADITIONAL LEMON MERINGUE PIE WITH NO WEEP MERINGUE

Serves 12

2 cups sugar

4 egg yolks (egg substitute is not recommended)

2 cups water

1/2 cup cornstarch

Dash salt

2 Tbsp. soft margarine

1/2 cup fresh-squeezed lemon juice

2 tsp. finely grated lemon peel

1 prepared 9-inch graham cracker crust

MERINGUE:

1 Tbsp. sugar

1 Tbsp. cornstarch

1/2 cup water

4 egg whites

1/4 cup sugar

In a medium saucepan, blend sugar, egg yolks, water, cornstarch, and salt. Cook until mixture thickens and clears. Remove from heat, and stir in margarine, lemon juice, and lemon peel. Pour in prepared pie crust. For meringue, cook sugar, cornstarch, and water in a medium saucepan, stirring constantly, until mixture is thick and clear. Set aside. In a glass bowl, beat 4 egg whites until frothy, slowly adding sugar. Continue beating until very stiff. Remove beater and fold in cooked cornstarch mixture. DO NOT BEAT THIS IN—fold gently. Spread meringue over lemon filling and bake for 12 minutes or until top of meringue is browned.

NUTRIENTS PER SERVING

275 calories, 7 gm. fat, 2 gm. saturated fat, 70 mg. cholesterol, 138 mg. sodium, 51 gm. carbohydrate, 2 gm. protein

Count as 2 1/2 fruit, 1 bread/starch, and 1 fat for food exchange eating plans.

20 minutes "hands-on" preparation time, 12 minutes baking time

Significant Symbols

MOTHER

On the second Sunday in May, mothers are the center of attention. Mother's Day has been officially recognized since President Woodrow Wilson proclaimed the day as "a public expression of our love and reverence for the mothers of our country" in 1914.

FATHER

On the third Sunday in June, fathers are truly "king for a day." In 1924, Calvin Coolidge recommended that Father's Day be noted in all states, declaring that celebration would bring about a clear relationship between fathers and their children.

ADD FUN, SUBTRACT EXPENSE

◆ *Before Mother's or Father's Day, ask all of the children of the family to write about their favorite memories of the parent of honor. Assemble these in a folder decorated with family pictures.*

◆ *Prepare your own card by writing about the qualities of your parent you are most thankful for.*

◆ *Consider the custom of wearing flowers on Mother's Day to honor your mother. Traditionally, you wear a pink carnation if your mother is alive and a white carnation if she is no longer alive.*

◆ Adopt the French custom of baking and decorating a Father's Day cake to serve at the end of the meal.

MENU IDEAS

KIDS MAKE BREAKFAST

Pineapple Orange French Toast

Grilled Ham

Kiwi and Strawberry Compote

Coffee

MOM OR DAD WILL LOVE THESE DINNER SUGGESTIONS

Chicken Margarita or Louisiana Stuffed Peppers or
Stir-Fried Sirloin and Spinach with Noodles

Fresh Green Salad with your favorite low-fat dressing
(dressing recipes are in Birthdays and Anniversaries chapter)

Blueberry Pecan Bread or Pineapple Blueberry Muffins

Rhubarb Cobbler

PINEAPPLE ORANGE FRENCH TOAST

Serves 4, 2 slices each

4 eggs or 1 cup liquid egg
  substitute

2/3 cup pineapple orange juice

1/3 cup skim milk

1 Tbsp. sugar

1 tsp. vanilla

1/8 tsp. nutmeg

8 slices sourdough bread

1 Tbsp. vegetable oil

In a medium mixing bowl, beat first 6 ingredients until blended. Arrange bread slices in a 9- by 13-inch pan. Pour egg mixture over bread. May cover and refrigerate for up to 24 hours, or bake immediately. Preheat oven to 400° F. Use a pastry brush to spread vegetable oil over a 15- by 8-inch baking sheet. Place bread in a single layer on pan. Bake for 20 minutes, and serve immediately with maple syrup.

NUTRIENTS PER SERVING

*196 calories, 5 gm. fat, 0 saturated fat, 0 cholesterol,
280 mg. sodium, 33 gm. carbohydrate, 5 gm. protein*

Count as 2 bread/starch and 1 fat for food exchange eating plans.

15 minutes "hands-on" preparation time, 20 minutes baking time

GRILLED HAM

ONLY 3 GRAMS OF FAT

Serves 4, 2 oz. each

8 oz. lean ham, cut into 4 slices   1 Tbsp. maple syrup

In a large skillet, heat syrup over medium heat. Add ham, and grill until lightly browned, about 2 minutes, on both sides. Serve with French toast.

NUTRIENTS PER SERVING

101 calories, 3 gm. fat, 1 gm. saturated fat, 31 mg. cholesterol, 751 mg. sodium (to reduce sodium, use low-sodium ham), 3 gm. carbohydrate, 14 gm. protein

Count as 2 lean meat for food exchange eating plans.

10 minutes "hands-on" preparation time, 4 minutes cooking time

KIWI AND STRAWBERRY COMPOTE

FAT-FREE!

Serves 8, 2/3 cup each

1 qt. fresh strawberries, washed, stemmed, and sliced thin

2 large kiwifruit, peeled and sliced thin

1/4 cup frozen pineapple juice concentrate

2 Tbsp. flaked coconut

Toss all ingredients in a salad bowl, and chill until serving.

NUTRIENTS PER SERVING

57 calories, 0 fat, 0 saturated fat, 0 cholesterol, 5 mg. sodium, 12 gm. carbohydrate, 0 gm. protein

Count as 1 fruit for food exchange eating plans.

15 minutes "hands-on" preparation time

CHICKEN MARGARITA

ONLY 3 GRAMS OF FAT

Serves 8

8 medium skinless, boneless
  chicken breast halves

1 tsp. ground coriander

1/4 tsp. salt

1/8 tsp. pepper

2 Tbsp. fresh-squeezed lime juice

1 Tbsp. cornstarch

1 tsp. sugar

1 cup no-added-salt chicken broth

1/2 cup orange juice

2 Tbsp. finely chopped cilantro

1 Tbsp. tequila

8 fresh lime slices

Rinse chicken, and pat it dry with paper towels. Combine coriander, salt, and pepper in a small bowl, and rub this mixture into the
chicken on both sides. Spray a cold large skillet with nonstick
cooking spray. Cook chicken in hot skillet for 8 to 10 minutes or
until tender and no longer pink. Remove chicken from the skillet
and keep warm. Combine lime juice, cornstarch, and sugar, and
set aside. Carefully add chicken broth and orange juice to the hot
skillet. Stir in lime juice mixture. Cook and stir until thickened
and bubbly. Cook for 1 more minute, then stir in cilantro and
tequila. Spoon sauce over the chicken. Garnish each chicken
breast with a fresh lime slice.

NUTRIENTS PER SERVING

*119 calories, 3 gm. fat, 1 gm. saturated fat, 45 mg. cholesterol,
377 mg. sodium, 4 gm. carbohydrate, 16 gm. protein*

Count as 2 lean meat for food exchange eating plans.

20 minutes "hands-on" preparation time, 15 minutes cooking time

LOUISIANA STUFFED PEPPERS

Serves 8

8 medium green peppers

1 lb. cooked roast beef, sliced into thin strips

1 small onion, finely chopped

1 /4 tsp. minced garlic

1/2 tsp. seasoned salt

1/2 tsp. cayenne pepper

2 oz. low-fat mozzarella cheese, shredded

3/4 cup dried bread crumbs

1 Tbsp. minced parsley

16-oz. can chunky tomatoes (do not drain)

1/2 tsp. oregano

1/2 tsp. basil

1/2 tsp. sugar

Preheat oven to 400° F. Cut off top of peppers. Remove seeds and membrane. In a mixing bowl, combine all remaining ingredients until well mixed. Stuff meat and tomato mixture into each pepper. Arrange peppers in a baking dish, and bake, covered, for 45 minutes. Uncover and bake for 15 more minutes.

NUTRIENTS PER SERVING

268 calories, 9 gm. fat, 3 gm. saturated fat, 49 mg. cholesterol, 440 mg. sodium, 27 gm. carbohydrate, 21 gm. protein

Count as 2 lean meat, 1 bread/starch, 1 vegetable, and 1 fat for food exchange eating plans.

15 minutes "hands-on" preparation time, 1 hour baking time

STIR-FRIED SIRLOIN AND SPINACH WITH NOODLES

Serves 8, 1 1/2 cups each

1 lb. boneless beef top sirloin
steak, cut 1 inch thick

8 oz. uncooked vermicelli

1 lb. fresh spinach, rinsed and
stems removed, thinly sliced

2 cups fresh bean sprouts

1 bunch green onions, washed,
trimmed, and diced

MARINADE:

1/3 cup reduced-sodium soy sauce

2 Tbsp. water

1/2 tsp. minced garlic

1/4 tsp. crushed red pepper

1/2 tsp. ground ginger

2 tsp. vegetable oil

Trim all fat from steak. First cut lengthwise and then crosswise into 1/8-inch thick strips. Combine marinade ingredients and pour half over beef. Cover and marinate in the refrigerator for at least 10 minutes. Reserve remaining marinade. Meanwhile, cook vermicelli according to package directions. Remove beef from marinade and discard marinade. Heat a large nonstick skillet over medium high heat until hot. Add the beef and stir-fry for 3 minutes over medium-high heat until cooked through. Remove from the skillet with a slotted spoon and keep warm. In the same skillet, combine vermicelli, spinach, bean sprouts, green onion, and reserved marinade. Cook for 3 minutes or until spinach is wilted and mixture is heated through. Return the beef to the skillet and mix with pasta and spinach.

NUTRIENTS PER SERVING

*307 calories, 10 gm. fat, 3 gm. saturated fat, 50 mg. cholesterol,
731 mg. sodium, 33 gm. carbohydrate, 20 gm. protein*

*Count as 2 lean meat, 1 1/2 bread/starch, 2 vegetable,
and 1/2 fat for food exchange eating plans*

*20 minutes "hands-on" preparation time,
10 minutes marinating time, 10 minutes cooking time*

BLUEBERRY PECAN BREAD

ONLY 3 GRAMS OF FAT

Serves 16, 1 slice each

2 cups flour, divided

2/3 cup sugar

1 1/2 tsp. baking powder

1/2 tsp. baking soda

1/2 tsp. salt

Juice and grated rind from
  1 lemon

2 Tbsp. soft margarine

1/2 cup boiling water

1 cup fresh blueberries, washed

1/4 cup chopped pecans

Preheat oven to 350° F. In a large mixing bowl, sift together 1 3/4 cups flour and dry ingredients. Pour lemon juice, rind, and margarine into a 1-cup measure. Add boiling water to make 3/4 cup. Stir liquid into dry ingredients, blending well. In a separate bowl, carefully combine berries, pecans, and remaining 1/4 cup flour. Fold berries into the batter, being careful not be mash them. Spoon batter into a large loaf pan that has been sprayed with nonstick cooking spray. Bake for 40 to 50 minutes or until bread tests done with a toothpick.

NUTRIENTS PER SERVING

*166 calories, 3 gm. fat, 0 saturated fat, 0 cholesterol,
123 mg. sodium, 32 gm. carbohydrate, 3 gm. protein*

Count as 1 bread/starch, 1 fruit, and 1/2 fat for food exchange eating plans.

15 minutes "hands-on" preparation time, 50 minutes baking time

PINEAPPLE BLUEBERRY MUFFINS

ONLY 1 GRAM OF FAT

Serves 12, 1 muffin each

1 Betty Crocker® wild blueberry
muffin mix

1 egg or 1/4 cup liquid
egg substitute

1/3 cup pineapple juice

2/3 cup crushed pineapple

Preheat oven to 425° F. Line 12 muffin cups with paper liners. Drain blueberries, rinse and set aside. Blend egg and juice in a medium bowl, using a fork. Add dry ingredients from the muffin mix. Stir just until flour is moistened. Fold in drained blueberries and pineapple just until blended. Bake for 20 minutes.

NUTRIENTS PER SERVING

*82 calories, 1 gm. fat, 0 saturated fat, 17 mg. cholesterol with egg
(0 with egg sub.), 5 mg. sodium, 15 gm. carbohydrate, 1 gm. protein*

Count as 1 bread/starch for food exchange eating plans.

15 minutes "hands-on" preparation time, 20 minutes baking time

RHUBARB COBBLER

ONLY 2 GRAMS OF FAT

Serves 8, 2/3 cup each

4 cups chopped rhubarb

2/3 cup sugar

3-oz. pkg. sugar-free raspberry
  gelatin mix

1 pkg. Jiffy® yellow cake mix

1 cup cran-raspberry juice

Preheat oven to 350° F. Spray a 9- by 13-inch cake pan with non-stick cooking spray. Sprinkle chopped rhubarb over the bottom of the pan. In a medium mixing bowl, combine sugar, gelatin, and cake mix. Sprinkle this mixture over the rhubarb. Pour cran-raspberry juice over the cake mix. Bake for 1 hour.

NUTRIENTS PER SERVING

*220 calories, 2 gm. fat, 0 saturated fat, 0 cholesterol,
236 mg. sodium, 50 gm. carbohydrate, 3 gm. protein*

Count as 2 bread/starch and 1 fruit for food exchange eating plans

15 minutes "hands-on" preparation time, 1 hour baking time

MEMORIAL DAY

Significant Symbols

HONORING HEROES

War heroes are remembered on May 30 or the last Monday in May, the official holiday. The custom of decorating graves with flowers was started in 1864 by Miss Emma Hunter who carried flowers to the tomb of her father, Colonel James Hunter, who commanded the 49th Pennsylvania Regiment that took part in the Battle of Gettysburg. For many years, the observance was known as Decoration Day.

PICNICS AND REUNIONS

The three-day Memorial Day weekend at the end of May has become the official start of summer in America and is marked by family reunions, graduation ceremonies, and backyard picnics.

ADD FUN, SUBTRACT EXPENSE

◆ *Trace your family history, and recount contributions of family members in the armed forces.*

◆ *Work together as a family to clean out winter clothes and coats. Consider giving away coats and wraps that haven't been worn that season.*

◆ *Attend a Memorial Day parade together.*

Menu Ideas

Saturday Night Grill-Out

Marinated Broiled Flank Steak

Black Bean and Jicama Salad

Hard rolls from the bakery or deli with low-fat margarine

Fruit Medley with Ricotta Dressing

Sunday Lunch

Open-Faced Steak Sandwiches or
Chicken Salad Olé

Zucchini Pasta Toss

Minted Summer Fruits

Lemon Chiffon Pie

MARINATED BROILED FLANK STEAK

Serves 8, 4 oz. each

1/4 cup reduced-sodium soy sauce
1/4 cup red wine vinegar
1 Tbsp. vegetable oil
2 tsp. Dijon-style mustard

1/2 tsp. crushed red pepper flakes
1 tsp. minced garlic
2 lb. flank steak

Combine soy sauce, vinegar, oil, mustard, pepper flakes, and minced garlic in a 1-gallon plastic bag that can be sealed and shaken. Slice the steak diagonally across the grain into 8 serving portions, and add them to the marinade. Refrigerate overnight. Preheat broiler. Remove steak from plastic bag and discard marinade. Broil the steak 3 inches from the heat for 5 minutes, then turn and broil for 4 more minutes or to desired doneness.

NUTRIENTS PER SERVING

256 calories, 13 gm. fat, 5 gm. saturated fat, 75 mg. cholesterol, 595 mg. sodium, 1 gm. carbohydrate, 31 gm. protein

Count as 4 lean meat and 1/2 fat for food exchange eating plans.

10 minutes "hands-on" preparation time, 12 hours marinating time, 10 minutes broiling time

BLACK BEAN AND JICAMA SALAD

ONLY 3 GRAMS OF FAT

Shelly Ahern found this recipe for our local dinner club.
Serves 8, 1 cup each

1-lb. can black beans, drained

10 oz. frozen whole-kernel corn, thawed and drained

3-oz. can diced green chiles, drained

2 cups finely diced jicama

1 large red pepper, finely diced

1/4 cup lime juice

1/4 cup vinegar

2 Tbsp. sugar

1 tsp. salt

1/2 tsp. black pepper

2 Tbsp. vegetable oil

1 tsp. cumin

Combine the first 5 ingredients in a large salad bowl. In a shaker container, combine remaining ingredients. Pour dressing over beans and vegetables, mix and chill for up to 24 hours, or serve immediately.

NUTRIENTS PER SERVING

201 calories, 3 gm. fat, 0 saturated fat, 0 cholesterol,
274 mg. sodium, 38 gm. carbohydrate, 6 gm. protein

Count as 1 vegetable, 2 bread/starch, and 1/2 fat for food exchange eating plans.

15 minutes "hands-on" preparation time

FRUIT MEDLEY WITH RICOTTA DRESSING

ONLY 2 GRAMS OF FAT

Serves 8, 2/3 cup each

2 pears, cored and chopped

1 small bunch green seedless grapes, cut in half

11-oz. can mandarin oranges, well drained

2 apples, cored and chopped

1 tsp. finely grated lemon rind

3 Tbsp. brown sugar

1 cup part-skim ricotta cheese

OPTIONAL GARNISH: 8 whole pecans

Combine fruits in a large salad bowl. In a blender container, combine lemon rind, brown sugar, and ricotta cheese. Blend until smooth, and use as a creamy dressing with fruits. Garnish individual fruit salads with a whole pecan.

NUTRIENTS PER SERVING

134 calories, 2 gm. fat, 1 gm. saturated fat, 9 mg. cholesterol, 41 mg. sodium, 25 gm. carbohydrate, 4 gm. protein

Count as 1 1/2 fruit and 1/2 skim milk for food exchange eating plans.

15 minutes "hands-on" preparation time

OPEN-FACED STEAK SANDWICHES

Serves 8

1 Tbsp. margarine, melted

3 Tbsp. reduced-sodium soy sauce

1 large red onion, thinly sliced

1/4 cup minced fresh parsley

1-lb. loaf Italian bread

1 lb. roast beef, thinly sliced

2 Tbsp. Romano cheese

Thoroughly blend margarine and soy sauce. Pour all but 2 Tbsp. of the mixture over onion and parsley in a small bowl, and stir to coat vegetables. Cut bread into 8 slices. Lightly brush both sides of bread with reserved soy sauce mixture. Place slices of bread on a baking sheet, and broil for 1 minute on both sides. Drain onion mixture, set aside. Cover each bread slice with roast beef, onion mixture, and Romano cheese. Return baking sheet to the broiler for 3 minutes. Serve immediately.

NUTRIENTS PER SERVING

317 calories, 10 gm. fat, 3 gm. saturated fat, 50 mg. cholesterol, 817 mg. sodium, 31 gm. carbohydrate, 22 gm. protein

Count as 2 bread/starch and 3 lean meat for food exchange eating plans.

15 minutes "hands-on" preparation time, 5 minutes broiling time

CHICKEN SALAD OLÉ

Serves 8, 2/3 cup each

8 flour tortillas	4 green onions, diced
Chili powder	1 yellow pepper, diced
1/2 cup fat-free sour cream	1/4 cup raisins
1/4 cup reduced-fat mayonnaise	1 head red-leaf lettuce, finely chopped
1 tsp. chili powder	
2 Tbsp. green chiles, well drained	**OPTIONAL DRESSING:** salsa
2 cups diced cooked chicken	

Preheat oven to 400° F. Lay out flour tortillas on 2 large baking sheets. Spray the tortillas with nonstick cooking spray. Sprinkle with chili powder. Bake for 10 minutes. Meanwhile, in a medium mixing bowl, combine sour cream, mayonnaise, chili powder, and green chiles. Mix well. Gently fold in chicken, onions, pepper and raisins. Remove tortillas from the oven, place on serving plates, and top with chopped lettuce and chicken salad. Serve salsa as a dressing on the side.

NUTRIENTS PER SERVING

278 calories, 8 gm. fat, 2 gm. saturated fat, 48 mg. cholesterol, 288 mg. sodium, 30 gm. carbohydrate, 23 gm. protein

Count as 1 1/2 bread/starch, 2 vegetable, and 2 lean meat for food exchange eating plans.

25 minutes "hands-on" preparation time, 10 minutes baking time

ZUCCHINI PASTA TOSS
ONLY 2 GRAMS OF FAT

Serves 8, 1 cup each

8 oz. shell pasta
3 fresh zucchini
1 Tbsp. vegetable oil
1/2 tsp. minced garlic
2 tsp. basil

1/4 cup freshly grated Parmesan cheese
1 tsp. lemon juice
1/4 tsp. salt
1/4 tsp. black pepper

In a large stockpot, cook pasta according to package directions. Be careful not to overcook. Rinse pasta with cold water immediately, and drain well. Meanwhile, shred zucchini. Combine cooked shells with zucchini in a large salad bowl. In a shaker container, combine remaining ingredients. Pour over pasta and vegetables, toss and serve.

NUTRIENTS PER SERVING

*75 calories, 2 gm. fat, 0 saturated fat, 11 mg. cholesterol,
114 mg. sodium, 9 gm. carbohydrate, 3 gm. protein*

*Count as 1/2 bread/starch and 1 vegetable
for food exchange eating plans.*

15 minutes "hands-on" preparation time, 15 minutes cooking time

MINTED SUMMER FRUITS
FAT-FREE!

Serves 8, 1 cup each

1/4 cup sugar

1/3 cup orange juice

1/3 cup ReaLemon® juice

1/3 cup water

1/4 tsp. peppermint extract

8 cups cut-up assorted fresh fruits of choice

(Note: 2 cups each apples, peaches, pears, and strawberries makes a nice combination.)

In a medium salad bowl, combine all ingredients except fruit. Stir until sugar dissolves. Gently fold fruits into the juice mixture. Cover and refrigerate until serving. This salad tastes just as good the second day because the lemon juice is a natural preservative.

NUTRIENTS PER SERVING

*132 calories, 0 fat, 0 saturated fat, 0 cholesterol, 3 mg. sodium,
33 gm. carbohydrate, 1 gm. protein*

Count as 2 fruit for food exchange eating plans.

15 minutes "hands-on" preparation time

LEMON CHIFFON PIE

Serves 12

8-oz. nonfat lemon yogurt

8-oz. reduced-fat cream cheese, softened

1/4 cup thawed white grape juice concentrate or 1 cup grape juice

2 tsp. finely grated lemon peel

2 cups reduced fat whipped topping

1 prepared 9-inch graham cracker crust

OPTIONAL GARNISH: fresh fruit of the season

In a medium mixing bowl, fold yogurt into softened cream cheese. Using an electric mixer on high power, blend grape juice concentrate and lemon peel into yogurt and cheese, beating for 2 minutes. Using a spatula, fold in whipped topping. Spoon into prepared crust and refrigerate for at least 2 hours. Slice and serve. Garnish with any fresh fruit.

NUTRIENTS PER SERVING

220 calories, 13 gm. fat, 6 gm. saturated fat, 7 mg. cholesterol, 236 mg. sodium, 21 gm. carbohydrate, 4 gm. protein

Count as 1 bread/starch, 1/2 fruit, and 2 1/2 fat for food exchange eating plans.

15 minutes "hands-on" preparation time, 2 hours chilling time

FLAG DAY

Significant Symbols

AMERICAN FLAG

Each year on June 14, flags are flown and honored as we celebrate the birthday of "Old Glory." In 1777, our flag was adopted, and a century later in 1877, Congress declared that it should be flown over public buildings annually on June 14.

ADD FUN, SUBTRACT EXPENSE

◆ *Purchase an American flag and display it outside your home.*

◆ *Say the Pledge of Allegiance as a table blessing.*

◆ *Play patriotic music like "The Stars and Stripes Forever," or "You're a Grand Old Flag" while you're making dinner.*

MENU IDEAS

Buttermilk Nectarine Blush

Honey Lime Chicken

Three Pepper Wild Rice Salad

Marinated Tomatoes

Red, White, and Blue Parfait

BUTTERMILK NECTARINE BLUSH

ONLY 1 GRAM OF FAT

Serves 8, 3/4 cup each

1 quart low-fat buttermilk

4 large nectarines, chilled, peeled, and cut into pieces

1/4 cup brown sugar

OPTIONAL GARNISH: diced fresh strawberries

Combine all ingredients in a blender container, blending until the nectarines are pureed. Serve in chilled glasses garnished with diced fresh strawberries.

NUTRIENTS PER SERVING

108 calories, 1 gm. fat, 0 saturated fat, 4 mg. cholesterol, 131 mg. sodium, 20 gm. carbohydrate, 4 gm. protein

Count as 1 fruit and 1/2 skim milk for food exchange eating plans.

10 minutes "hands-on" preparation time

HONEY LIME CHICKEN

ONLY 1 GRAM OF FAT

Thanks to Nancy McGraw and Tones® spices.

Serves 8

20-oz. can chunk pineapple

8 boneless, skinless chicken breast halves

1 tsp. Tone's granulated garlic

4 Tbsp. lime or lemon juice

2 Tbsp. reduced sodium soy sauce

2 tsp. cornstarch

1/4 tsp. honey

Drain pineapple, reserving 2 tablespoons of juice. Sprinkle chicken with garlic. Broil or grill chicken until cooked through, about 4-6 minutes on each side with medium-high heat. Combine reserved pineapple juice, lime juice, soy sauce, cornstarch, and honey in a saucepan. Cook over medium heat, stirring, until thick. Add pineapple to sauce, and heat through. Spoon sauce and pineapple over grilled chicken.

NUTRIENTS PER SERVING

142 calories, 1 gm. fat, 0 saturated fat, 44 mg. cholesterol, 225 mg. sodium, 14 gm. carbohydrate, 17 gm. protein

Count as 1 1/2 meat and 1 fruit for food exchange eating plans.

20 minutes "hands-on" preparation time, 20 minutes cooking time

THREE PEPPER AND WILD RICE SALAD
FAT-FREE!

Serves 8, 3/4 cup each

6-oz. pkg. long-grain wild rice
1/2 cup reduced-fat mayonnaise
1/2 tsp. black pepper
1/2 tsp. finely grated lemon peel

1 large yellow pepper, chopped
1 large green pepper, chopped
1 large red pepper, chopped

Prepare rice as directed on the package, omitting margarine. Cool and combine rice with mayonnaise, black pepper, and lemon peel. Add chopped peppers. Mix lightly, serve at room temperature or chilled.

NUTRIENTS PER SERVING

49 calories, 0 fat, 0 saturated fat, 0 cholesterol, 181 mg. sodium, 11 gm. carbohydrate, 1 gm. protein

Count as 1/2 bread/starch and 1/2 vegetable for food exchange eating plans.

15 minutes "hands-on" preparation time, 40 minutes cooking time

MARINATED TOMATOES

ONLY 2 GRAMS OF FAT

Serves 8, 1/2 cup each

6 large tomatoes
1/4 cup sliced black olives
4 green onions, diced
1 Tbsp. vegetable oil

2 Tbsp. red-wine vinegar
1/8 tsp. seasoned salt
1/4 tsp. black pepper

Core tomatoes and slice thin onto a serving plate. Combine remaining ingredients in a small mixing bowl. Pour over tomato slices, cover, and refrigerate for at least 30 minutes.

NUTRIENTS PER SERVING

46 calories, 2 gm. fat, 0 saturated fat, 0 cholesterol, 102 mg. sodium, 5 gm. carbohydrate, 0 protein

Count as 1 vegetable and 1/2 fat for food exchange eating plans.

15 minutes "hands-on" preparation time, 30 minutes chilling time

....

RED, WHITE, AND BLUE PARFAIT

ONLY 1 GRAM OF FAT

Serves 8, 3/4 cup each

2 cups frozen raspberries

1/3 cup all-fruit raspberry jam

15 oz. fat-free ricotta cheese

1/4 cup powdered sugar

2 cups blueberries

1/2 cup reduced-fat granola

Combine raspberries with jam in a small mixing bowl. In a blender container, combine ricotta with sugar. Divide and layer into parfait glasses: 1/3 ricotta mixture, raspberry mixture, 1/3 ricotta mixture, fresh blueberries, 1/3 ricotta mixture, and top with granola. Chill for at least 30 minutes or up to overnight.

NUTRIENTS PER SERVING

*173 calories, 1 gm. fat, 0 saturated fat, 18 mg. cholesterol,
85 mg. sodium, 36 gm. carbohydrate, 8 gm. protein*

*Count as 1 fruit, 1 bread/starch, and 1/2 skim milk
for food exchange eating plans.*

15 minutes "hands-on" preparation time, 30 minutes chilling time

FOURTH OF JULY

Significant Symbols

DECLARATION OF INDEPENDENCE

On July 4, 1776, the Continental Congress assembled in Philadelphia and announced that it had become independent from the mother country, England. The nation's proudest secular holiday commemorates the birth of our nation, and no matter what part of the globe Americans find themselves in, they observe this important date.

FIREWORKS

Fireworks were used as early as 1788 to celebrate this national holiday. Parades, patriotic plays, bell-ringing, flag displays, and marching bands keep the spirit of nationalism alive today.

ADD FUN, SUBTRACT EXPENSE

◆ *Organize your own neighborhood parade with walkers dressing in red, white, and blue and bikers decorating their two-wheelers with streamers.*

◆ *Ask an older child to read aloud from the Declaration of Independence as a table blessing.*

◆ *Purchase some red, white, and blue fabric, and line your picnic basket with it for the day.*

MENU IDEAS

STAR SPANGLED PICNIC #1

Strawberry-Lemon Slush

All American Beef Kabobs on the Grill

Not-Your-Mother's Baked Beans

Creamy Low-fat Potato Salad

Stars and Stripes Dessert

STAR SPANGLED PICNIC # 2

Gazpacho

Mustard Glazed Chicken

Cornmeal Muffins with Onions and Chives

All-American Vegetable Salad

Home Frozen Ice Cream with
Fresh Blueberries and Strawberries

STRAWBERRY-LEMON SLUSH

FAT-FREE!

Serves 8, 3/4 cup each

2 cups water
1 cup lemon juice
1/2 cup sugar
2 cups fresh strawberries

1 cup crushed ice
Red food coloring
OPTIONAL GARNISH: fresh lemon slices

Put 1 cup of the water, lemon juice, sugar, and berries in a blender container. Blend until berries are pureed and the sugar is dissolved. In a glass pitcher, combine strawberry mixture with remaining water, crushed ice and a few drops of red food coloring. Serve in short cocktail glasses garnished with lemon slices. For a carbonated slush, mix half and half with sugar-free lemon lime soft drink or sparkling wine.

NUTRIENTS PER SERVING

65 calories, 0 fat, 0 saturated fat, 0 cholesterol, 6 mg. sodium, 16 gm. carbohydrate, 0 protein

Count as 1 fruit for food exchange eating plans.

15 minutes "hands-on" preparation time

ALL AMERICAN BEEF KABOBS ON THE GRILL

Serves 8, 1 kabob each

1/2 cup reduced-sodium soy sauce

2 Tbsp. vegetable oil

1 Tbsp. dark corn syrup or maple syrup

1/2 tsp. minced garlic

1 tsp. dry mustard

1 tsp. ground ginger

2 lb. beef sirloin steak, cut into 1 1/2-inch pieces

3 green peppers, cut in 1-inch squares

4 small, firm tomatoes, quartered

1 small yellow onion, quartered and peeled into wedges

Combine first 6 ingredients in a large bowl. Add sirloin, and marinate in the refrigerator for 30 minutes or overnight. Drain meat. Alternate meat, pepper, tomato, and onion on skewers. Grill over medium-hot coals until desired doneness, allowing 15 minutes for rare.

NUTRIENTS PER SERVING

318 calories, 14 gm. fat, 4 gm. saturated fat, 94 mg. cholesterol, 1051 mg. sodium (to reduce sodium, use 1/4 cup reduced-sodium soy sauce and 1/4 cup red wine), 11 gm. carbohydrate, 34 gm. protein

Count as 4 lean meat, 2 vegetable, and 1 fat for food exchange eating plans.

15 minutes "hands-on" preparation time, 30 minutes marinating time, 15 minutes grilling time

NOT-YOUR-MOTHER'S BAKED BEANS

ONLY 2 GRAMS OF FAT

Serves 8, 1/2 cup each

4 slices bacon, diced

16-oz. can pork and beans

1 green pepper, chopped

1 large yellow onion, chopped

1/4 cup catsup

1/4 cup brown sugar

1 Tbsp. dry mustard

1/2 tsp. black pepper

1/4 tsp. cloves

1/8 tsp. cinnamon

Preheat oven to 350° F. Cook bacon until very crisp, then drain well. Combine diced cooked bacon with remaining ingredients in a 2-quart baking dish. Bake uncovered for 1 1/2 hours. If it is a hot day, use the crockpot, uncovered, on high heat for 2 hours.

NUTRIENTS PER SERVING

127 calories, 2 gm. fat, 0 saturated fat, 2 mg. cholesterol, 139 mg. sodium, 22 gm. carbohydrate, 5 gm. protein

Count as 1 1/2 bread/starch for food exchange eating plans.

15 minutes "hands-on" preparation time, 1 hour and 30 minutes baking time or 2 hours crockpot time

CREAMY LOW-FAT POTATO SALAD

ONLY 2 GRAMS OF FAT

Serves 8, 3/4 cup each

4 large red potatoes, boiled until tender and diced

4 hard boiled eggs, diced

4 green onions, diced

1 cup nonfat mayonnaise

1/3 cup buttermilk

1 Tbsp. Dijon-style or prepared yellow mustard

1/8 tsp. black pepper

OPTIONAL GARNISHES:

minced fresh parsley or paprika

In a large salad bowl, combine cooked potatoes, hard boiled eggs, and diced onions. In a small bowl, combine mayonnaise, buttermilk, mustard, and black pepper. Pour dressing over potatoes and gently stir to mix. Cover and refrigerate until service. Garnish with minced fresh parsley or paprika.

NUTRIENTS PER SERVING

135 calories, 2 gm. fat, 0 saturated fat, 106 mg. cholesterol, 128 mg. sodium, 22 gm. carbohydrate, 5 gm. protein

Count as 1 1/2 bread/starch and 1/2 fat for food exchange eating plans.

15 minutes "hands-on" preparation time, 25 minutes cooking time for potatoes, 20 minutes cooking time for eggs

• •

STARS AND STRIPES DESSERT

Serves 24

1 94% fat-free white cake mix
Water
3 eggs or 3/4 cup egg substitute
2/3 cup nonfat ricotta cheese
2 Tbsp. powdered sugar

2 cups reduced-fat whipped
  topping
1 qt. fresh strawberries
2 cups fresh blueberries

Spray a 15- by 8-inch jelly-roll pan with nonstick cooking spray. Prepare white cake mix with water and eggs according to package directions, and pour into pan. Bake for 20 to 25 minutes or until cake tests done with a toothpick. When cake is done, run a knife around the edges, then let the cake cool. In a medium mixing bowl, beat ricotta with powdered sugar until smooth. Fold in whipped topping. When cake is cool, pour all of the topping on the cake and spread evenly. Rinse, core, and slice strawberries in half vertically, then blot dry on a paper towel. Rinse blueberries and pour onto paper towel to dry. With a knife, mark a rectangle in the upper left corner of the topping, 5 inches wide by 3 inches deep. Fill this with blueberries to form the star portion of the American flag. To form stripes, start at the top of the cake next to the blueberries, and make 2 rows of strawberries very close to each other. Then make another 2 rows of strawberries across the bottom of the cake. Do a third double row in the center of the cake, starting just under the blueberries. This dessert makes a pretty centerpiece for a Fourth of July gathering.

NUTRIENTS PER SERVING

*157 calories, 4 gm. fat, 2 gm. saturated fat, 1 mg. cholesterol,
159 mg. sodium, 28 gm. carbohydrate, 3 gm. protein*

Count as 1 fruit, 1 bread/starch, and 1/2 fat for food exchange eating plans.

25 minutes "hands-on" preparation time, 25 minutes baking time

GAZPACHO

FAT-FREE!

Serves 8, 1 cup each

1 large cucumber

2 firm medium-size tomatoes, cored and quartered

2 stalks celery

2 carrots, peeled and trimmed

1 red pepper, cored and seeds removed

1 green pepper, cored and seeds removed

4 cups tomato juice

1 Tbsp. vinegar

1 Tbsp. lime juice

1 tsp. cumin

GARNISH: celery leaves

Puree vegetables individually in a food processor or chopper to desired texture. I prefer a consistency similar to chunky salsa. Combine pureed vegetables in a large bowl. Stir in remaining ingredients, then cover and refrigerate until service. Garnish the top of the gazpacho with celery leaves.

NUTRIENTS PER SERVING

44 calories, 0 fat, 0 saturated fat, 0 cholesterol, 428 mg. sodium, 10 gm. carbohydrate, 1 gm. protein

Count as 2 vegetable for food exchange eating plans.

20 minutes "hands-on" preparation time

MUSTARD GLAZED CHICKEN

ONLY 3 GRAMS OF FAT

Serves 8, 1 half chicken breast each

4 whole chicken breasts, boned,
  skinned and cut in half

1/2 cup prepared mustard

3 Tbsp. lime juice

2 Tbsp. honey or maple syrup

1/2 cup water

1 tsp. ground coriander

2 tsp. grated lime peel

Preheat oven to 350° F. Place chicken breasts in a shallow baking pan. Whisk together remaining ingredients. Pour mustard mixture over the chicken. Bake for 30 minutes, uncovered, until chicken is done.

NUTRIENTS PER SERVING

*155 calories, 3 gm. fat, 0 saturated fat, 73 mg. cholesterol,
247 mg. sodium, 5 gm. carbohydrate, 26 gm. protein*

Count as 2 1/2 lean meat and 1/2 fruit for food exchange eating plans.

10 minutes "hands-on" preparation time, 30 minutes baking time

CORNMEAL MUFFINS WITH ONIONS AND CHIVES

ONLY 2 GRAMS OF FAT

Serves 12, 1 large muffin each

2 envelopes cornmeal muffin mix
2 eggs or 1/2 cup liquid egg
  substitute
1/2 cup buttermilk

1 Tbsp. dried onion
1/4 cup chopped fresh chives

Preheat oven to 400° F. Prepare two envelopes of cornmeal muffin mix according to package directions, with eggs, using buttermilk for the liquid. Fold in dried onion and chives. Spoon batter into 12 prepared muffin cups. Bake for 15 to 20 minutes or until muffins test done with a toothpick.

NUTRIENTS PER SERVING

146 calories, 2 gm. fat, 0 saturated fat, 35 mg. cholesterol with egg (1 mg. with egg sub.), 21 mg. sodium, 26 gm. carbohydrate, 3 gm. protein

Count as 2 bread/starch for food exchange eating plans.

10 minutes "hands-on" preparation time, 20 minutes baking time

ALL AMERICAN VEGETABLE SALAD

Pat Burroughs served this at a summer party.
Serves 16, 1 cup each

11-oz. can bean sprouts, drained
8-oz. can mushrooms, drained
8-oz. can sliced water chestnuts, drained
1 green pepper, diced

1 red pepper, diced
1 small yellow onion, diced
1/2 head cauliflower, separated into flowerets
2 stalks celery, diced

DRESSING:

1/3 cup vegetable oil
1/3 cup water
1 cup sugar
1/2 cup white vinegar

1 Tbsp. prepared mustard
1/4 tsp. salt
1/4 tsp. black pepper

Combine vegetables in a large salad bowl. In a shaker container, mix ingredients for dressing. Pour dressing over vegetables and stir gently. Cover and refrigerate 24 hours for best flavor.

NUTRIENTS PER SERVING

122 calories, 4 gm. fat, 0 saturated fat, 0 cholesterol,
49 mg. sodium, 20 gm. carbohydrate, 1 gm. protein

Count as 3 vegetable and 1 fat for food exchange eating plans.

25 minutes "hands-on" preparation time, 24 hours chilling time

HOME FROZEN ICE CREAM WITH FRESH BLUEBERRIES AND STRAWBERRIES

Serves 16, 1/2 cup each

5 eggs, beaten	2 Tbsp. vanilla
3 Tbsp. flour	1 1/2 qt. whole milk
1/4 tsp. salt	1 pt. half and half
2 cups sugar	Fresh blueberries and strawberries
1 1/4 cups whole milk	

In a medium saucepan, combine beaten eggs, flour, salt, and sugar. Whisk in 1 1/4 cups whole milk. Cook over medium heat, stirring constantly until mixture is thickened and clear. Pour cooked mixture into the freezing container of a manual or electric ice cream freezer. Stir in vanilla, whole milk, and half and half. Layer crushed ice and rock salt around freezing container. Manually turn or process electrically until ice cream is semi-solid. Serve ice cream with fresh blueberries and strawberries.

NUTRIENTS PER SERVING

213 calories, 5 gm. fat, 3 gm. saturated fat, 83 mg. cholesterol, 123 mg. sodium, 34 gm. carbohydrate, 6 gm. protein

Count as 1 skim milk, 1 1/2 fruit, and 1 fat for food exchange eating plans.

15 minutes "hands-on" preparation time, 30 minutes freezing time

Significant Symbols

HONORING WORKERS

The idea to honor American workers was first suggested in 1882 by Peter J. McGuire, the president of the United Brotherhood of Carpenters. By 1894, it was a legal holiday in most states. The celebration of the rights and accomplishments of workers continues to this day in the form of speeches by labor leaders, family picnics, athletic events, and parades.

ADD FUN, SUBTRACT EXPENSE

◆ *As Labor Day marks the beginning of the school year and the end of summer, organize one last softball game, picnic on the beach, or trip to an outdoor antique mall.*

◆ *Make a game of a family research project. Get out the family tree and discuss what your ancestors did for their life's work.*

MENU IDEAS

WEEKEND GRILL-OUT

Minty Pear Punch

Nectarine Salsa with Low-Fat Chips

Turkey Steaks Cantonese

Creamy Nonfat Coleslaw

Fall Garden Casserole

Apricot Bundt® Cake

MONDAY BREAKFAST

Orange-Pineapple Frappé

Oven Eggs Benedict

Zucchini Bread

MINTY PEAR PUNCH

FAT-FREE!

Serves 8, 1 cup each

46-oz. can pineapple juice   2 tsp. lemon juice
17-oz. can pear halves in juice   Peppermint extract

Pour 1 cup pineapple juice into a blender container. Add pear halves and juice. Process until smooth. Combine pureed pears with remaining pineapple juice, lemon juice, and a few drops of peppermint extract in a 2 1/2-qt. serving pitcher. Pour into short tumblers, and garnish glasses with fresh mint leaves.

NUTRIENTS PER SERVING

*133 calories, 0 fat, 0 saturated fat, 0 cholesterol,
4 mg. sodium, 33 gm. carbohydrate, 1 gm. protein*

Count as 2 fruit for food exchange eating plans.

15 minutes "hands-on" preparation time

NECTARINE SALSA WITH LOW-FAT CHIPS

FAT-FREE!

Serves 8, 1/3 cup each

1 ripe nectarine, chopped   1/2 tsp. chili powder
4 green onions, diced   2 banana or Hungarian hot wax
2 firm ripe tomatoes, chopped   peppers, diced (Note: always
1 1/2 Tbsp. chopped fresh mint   wear rubber gloves when han-
                                      dling hot peppers.)

Combine all ingredients in a medium glass bowl. Cover, refriger-ate, and serve with reduced-fat tortilla chips.

149

NUTRIENTS PER SERVING

*22 calories, 0 fat, 0 saturated fat, 0 cholesterol,
3 mg. sodium, 5 gm. carbohydrate, 0 protein*

Count as 1 vegetable for food exchange eating plans.

15 minutes "hands-on" preparation time

TURKEY STEAKS CANTONESE

ONLY 2 GRAMS OF FAT

Serves 8, 4 oz. each

2 tsp. vegetable oil

2 lb. turkey breast, cut into
8 4-oz. steaks

6-oz. can pineapple juice

1/2 cup chicken or turkey broth

1/4 tsp. minced garlic

2 1/2 Tbsp. reduced-sodium
soy sauce

1/4 tsp. fennel

1 tsp. sugar

1 large red onion, cut in half and
thinly sliced

1 medium green pepper, quartered
and sliced 1/8-inch thick

2 Tbsp. diced pimiento

In a large skillet, heat oil over medium heat. Sear both sides of the
turkey steaks quickly. Remove to a plate. Add juice, broth, and
garlic to the skillet. Boil for 8 minutes to reduce volume by half.
Add soy sauce, fennel, sugar, and vegetables. Simmer for 2 minutes
or until vegetables start to soften. Return steaks to the skillet.
Spoon mixture over the steaks and simmer for 4 to 6 minutes until
steaks are no longer pink. Remove steaks to a platter, cover with
onion mixture, and serve hot.

CREAMY NONFAT COLESLAW
FAT-FREE!

Serves 8, 1 cup each

1 lb. shredded cabbage and carrots   1 small yellow onion, diced
2 stalks celery, finely diced

DRESSING:

1 cup nonfat mayonnaise   1 Tbsp. sugar
1/2 cup buttermilk   1 Tbsp. vinegar
1/4 tsp. black pepper

Combine vegetables in a large salad bowl. In a small mixing bowl, whisk together ingredients for dressing. Pour dressing over vegetables, cover and refrigerate for up to 4 hours before service.

NUTRIENTS PER SERVING

*73 calories, 0 fat, 0 saturated fat, 0 cholesterol,
408 mg. sodium, 16 gm. carbohydrate, 2 gm. protein*

Count as 3 vegetable for food exchange eating plans.

15 minutes "hands-on" preparation time

FALL GARDEN CASSEROLE

Serves 8, 1 cup each

1/4 cup slivered almonds	1 tsp. garlic, minced
4 slices bacon, diced	1 tsp. basil
4 medium zucchini, sliced thin	1/4 tsp. salt
1 large onion, cut in wedges	1/4 tsp. pepper
2 large fresh tomatoes, seeded and chopped	2 oz. reduced-fat Swiss cheese, shredded
1 Tbsp. flour	

Preheat oven to 400° F. In a large skillet, sauté almonds with diced bacon. When bacon is cooked crisp, remove almonds and bacon to a small bowl. In a 3-quart baking dish, layer zucchini, onion, and tomatoes. In a small mixing bowl, combine flour, garlic, basil, salt, and pepper. Fold this mixture into the vegetables. Spread cheese over top of vegetables, and sprinkle with reserved almonds and bacon. Bake for 20 minutes. To microcook, cook on high heat for 12 to 15 minutes.

NUTRIENTS PER SERVING

98 calories, 6 gm. fat, 1 gm. saturated fat, 6 mg. cholesterol, 211 mg. sodium, 9 gm. carbohydrate, 5 gm. protein

Count as 2 vegetable and 1 fat for food exchange eating plans.

15 minutes "hands-on" preparation time, 20 minutes baking time

APRICOT BUNDT® CAKE

ONLY 2 GRAMS OF FAT

Serves 24

1 94% fat-free yellow cake mix
1 1/3 cups apricot nectar
3 eggs or 3/4 cup egg substitute
1 tsp. cinnamon

1/2 tsp. ground nutmeg
1/2 cup finely shredded
  dried apricots
OPTIONAL GARNISH: sifted
  powdered sugar

Preheat oven to 350° F. Combine first three ingredients in a large mixing bowl. Beat on low power for 1 minute, scraping the bowl often. Beat 2 more minutes on high power. Spray a Bundt pan with nonstick cooking spray. Pour half of the batter into the pan. Sprinkle cinnamon, nutmeg, and shredded apricots over batter. Pour remaining half of batter into the pan, spreading evenly with a spatula. Bake for 45 minutes or until cake tests done with a toothpick. Cool for 20 minutes, then turn out onto a serving plate. If desired, garnish slices of cake with sifted powdered sugar.

NUTRIENTS PER SERVING

*109 calories, 2 gm. fat, 0 saturated fat, 27 mg. cholesterol
(0 with egg sub.), 164 mg. sodium,
21 gm. carbohydrate, 2 gm. protein*

Count as 1 1/2 bread/starch for food exchange eating plans

*15 minutes "hands-on" preparation time,
45 minutes baking time, 20 minutes cooling time*

ORANGE-PINEAPPLE FRAPPÉ

ONLY 1 GRAM OF FAT

Serves 8, 1/2 cup each

1 cup orange sherbet

3 cups pineapple-orange juice

OPTIONAL GARNISH: fresh pineapple wedges

Combine sherbet and juice in a 2-quart blender container. Process on medium speed until well blended. Pour out into juice glasses or wine goblets. Garnish glasses with fresh pineapple wedges.

NUTRIENTS PER SERVING

91 calories, 1 gm. fat, 0 saturated fat, 2 mg. cholesterol, 14 mg. sodium, 22 gm. carbohydrate, 1 gm. protein

Count as 1 1/2 fruit for food exchange eating plans.

5 minutes "hands-on" preparation time

OVEN EGGS BENEDICT

Serves 8, 2 muffin halves each

8 English muffins, sliced in half

16 1-oz. slices lean Canadian bacon

2 large, firm tomatoes, sliced into 8 thin slices each

4 hard boiled eggs, diced

1 Tbsp. soft margarine

2 Tbsp. flour

1 1/2 cups skim milk

1/4 tsp. salt

1/4 tsp. white pepper

1 Tbsp. prepared mustard

Arrange muffin halves on 2 large baking sheets. Put a slice of Canadian bacon and a slice of tomato on each half. Sprinkle diced eggs over tomatoes. Melt margarine in a small saucepan. Stir in flour. Using a whisk, stir in skim milk, and cook over medium heat until mixture is thick. Stir in salt, pepper, and mustard. Pour white sauce over muffins. Place under broiler for 5 minutes and serve.

NUTRIENTS PER SERVING

340 calories, 12 gm. fat, 3 gm. saturated fat, 161 mg. cholesterol, 459 mg. sodium, 32 gm. carbohydrate, 26 gm. protein

Count as 2 bread/starch and 3 lean meat for food exchange eating plans.

20 minutes "hands-on" preparation time, 5 minutes broiling time

ZUCCHINI BREAD

Serves 24, 1 slice each

3 cups flour
1 1/2 tsp. salt
1 Tbsp. ground cinnamon
1 tsp. baking soda
1/2 tsp. baking powder
1 cup sugar
1/2 cup vegetable oil

1/2 cup nonfat sour cream
3 eggs or 3/4 cup liquid egg substitute
1 tsp. vanilla
1 tsp. finely grated orange rind
3 cups shredded zucchini

Preheat oven to 350° F. Spray 2 loaf pans with nonstick cooking spray. In a large mixing bowl, combine first 5 ingredients. In another medium bowl, whisk together sugar, oil, sour cream, eggs, vanilla, and rind. Stir into flour mixture. Fold in zucchini. Pour into prepared pans, and bake for 45 to 50 minutes or until breads test done. Remove from pans to wire rack to cool.

NUTRIENTS PER SERVING

140 calories, 5 gm. fat, 1 gm. saturated fat,
26 mg. cholesterol (0 with egg sub.),
206 mg. sodium, 21 gm. carbohydrate, 3 gm. protein

Count as 1 bread/starch, 1/2 fruit, and 1 fat for food exchange eating plans.

15 minutes "hands-on" preparation time, 50 minutes baking time

Significant Symbols

MEDITATION AND SELF-EXAMINATION

Rosh Hashanah, meaning "head," or beginning of the New Year, occurs on the first day of the Jewish month of Tishri. The date ranges from September 6 to October 5. Jews start the religious year, not with gaiety but with thoughtful reflection and sorrow for wrongs committed. Rosh Hashanah marks the beginning of a ten-day observance that is climaxed by Yom Kippur, the Day of Atonement. Jewish adults fast and spend the day in the synagogue to make amends for their sins .

SWEETS AT SUNDOWN

Traditionally, as the new year begins, Jewish people eat sweet foods at sundown to symbolize their wish for a "sweet" year.

MENU IDEAS

Apple Honey Oatmeal Cookies

Aunt Rose's Honey Cookies

Rose Robinson's Honey Cake with Coffee

Grammy's Pecan Rolls

Ziggy's Challah

APPLE HONEY OATMEAL COOKIES

ONLY 2 GRAMS OF FAT

Serves 72, 1 small cookie each

3/4 cup margarine

1 1/4 cups firmly packed, light brown sugar

1 egg or 1/4 cup liquid egg substitute

1/3 cup skim milk

2 Tbsp. honey

1 1/2 tsp. vanilla

3 cups quick cooking oats, uncooked

1 cup all-purpose flour

1/2 tsp. baking soda

1/2 tsp. salt

1/2 tsp. cinnamon

1 cup raisins

1/4 cup chopped walnuts

1 Granny Smith apple, peeled, cored, and finely chopped

Preheat oven to 375° F. Spray baking sheets with nonstick cooking spray. In a large mixing bowl, cream margarine with brown sugar. Beat in egg. Beat in milk, honey, and vanilla. In a medium mixing bowl, combine oats, flour, baking soda, salt and cinnamon. Add oatmeal mixture to creamed mixture, mixing at low speed just until blended. Fold in raisins, nuts, and apple. Drop by spoonfuls onto baking sheets. Bake for 12 minutes or until lightly browned. Cool for 2 minutes on the baking sheet before removing to a cooling rack.

NUTRIENTS PER SERVING

70 calories, 2 gm. fat, 0 saturated fat, 2 mg. cholesterol with egg (0 with egg sub.), 42 mg. sodium, 11 gm. carbohydrate, 1 gm. protein

Count as 1 bread/starch for food exchange eating plans.

20 minutes "hands-on" preparation time, 12 minutes baking time

AUNT ROSE'S HONEY COOKIES

ONLY 1 GRAM OF FAT

Serves 72, 1 small cookie each

1 cup sugar

2 Tbsp. vegetable oil

1 tsp. baking powder

1/2 tsp. baking soda

3 large eggs or 3/4 cup liquid
egg substitute

1/4 tsp. salt

1 Tbsp. grated lemon rind

1 cup honey

2 tsp. allspice

1 tsp. ground ginger

1/2 cup white raisins

1/4 cup chopped walnuts

2 3/4 cups flour

Preheat oven to 350° F. Beat together sugar, oil, baking powder, baking soda, eggs, and salt for 10 minutes with electric mixer at medium speed. Add lemon rind, honey, allspice, ginger, raisins, walnuts, and flour. Stir to mix. Turn dough onto floured board. If mixture is too sticky to work with, add 1/8 cup flour. Make small balls of cookie dough, using about 1 Tbsp. per cookie. Place on baking sheets that have been sprayed with nonstick cooking spray. Bake for 12 minutes. Cookies will be brown on the edges and lighter in the center.

NUTRIENTS PER SERVING

69 calories, 1 gm. fat, 1 gm. saturated fat, 1 mg. cholesterol with egg (0 with egg sub.), 18 mg. sodium, 15 gm. carbohydrate, 2 gm. protein

Count as 1 bread/starch for food exchange eating plans.

20 minutes "hands-on" preparation time, 12 minutes baking time

ROSE ROBINSON'S HONEY CAKE WITH COFFEE

ONLY 3 GRAMS OF FAT

Serves 20

1/3 cup reduced-fat margarine	3/4 tsp. salt
1 cup sugar	1/4 tsp. ginger
2 large eggs or 1/2 cup liquid egg substitute	1/2 tsp. cinnamon
	1/2 tsp. cloves
1/3 cup honey	1/2 tsp. allspice
1 1/2 tsp. grated lemon rind	1/2 cup strong coffee
2 cups flour	1/3 cup raisins
1 tsp. baking powder	2 Tbsp. chopped walnuts
3/4 tsp. baking soda	

Preheat oven to 350° F. In a large bowl, cream margarine and sugar until well blended. Add eggs one at a time, and beat for 1 minute after each addition. Add honey and lemon rind. In another bowl, mix together flour, baking powder, baking soda, salt, and spices, and add alternately with coffee to egg mixture. Blend well. Stir in raisins. Turn into loaf pan that has been sprayed with nonstick cooking spray. Sprinkle top of loaf with chopped walnuts. Bake for 40 to 45 minutes or until cake tests done. Cool 10 minutes, then turn cake out of loaf pan and cool on a wire rack. Cut loaf into 10 slices, then cut each slice in half to serve.

NUTRIENTS PER SERVING

172 calories, 3 gm. fat, 0 saturated fat, 2 mg. cholesterol with egg (0 with egg sub.), 167 mg. sodium, 38 gm. carbohydrate, 3 gm. protein

Count as 1 bread/starch, 1 fruit, and 1/2 fat for food exchange eating plans.

20 minutes "hands-on" preparation time, 45 minutes baking time

GRAMMY'S PECAN ROLLS

These rolls are meant to be started at night and baked the next day.
This recipe is courtesy of Fanny Kasnow.
Serves 48, 1 mini-muffin size roll each

2 1/2 cups flour	1/4 cup soft reduced-fat margarine
1/2 cup sugar	1/3 cup brown sugar
1/2 cup skim milk	48 pecan halves
1/2 cup soft reduced-fat margarine	2 Tbsp. reduced fat margarine, melted
1 pkg. dry quick-acting yeast	
1 tsp. sugar	Flour
1/4 cup hot water	1/2 cup cinnamon sugar (1/3 cup sugar plus 3 Tbsp. cinnamon)
2 eggs or 1/2 cup liquid egg substitute	1 cup white raisins

In a large bowl, mix flour and sugar. In a small saucepan, combine milk and margarine, and heat until margarine melts; do not boil. Mix dry yeast with 1 tsp. sugar in 1/4 cup hot water. Stir and let it come to froth. Make a well in the flour and sugar mixture, and pour yeast mixture into the well. Beat eggs well and add to bowl. Add milk and margarine mixture and beat well. Cover the dish with a towel and allow to rest in a cool place overnight. In the morning, preheat the oven to 400° F. Spray each mini-muffin cup with nonstick cooking spray. Drop 1/2 tsp. reduced-fat margarine and 1 tsp. brown sugar into each one. Press one pecan half into each muffin cup, flat side up. Spread flour onto a work surface. Divide dough into three parts. Roll each third separately into 14- by 9-inch rectangles. Brush melted margarine across the top of the rectangles. Sprinkle each rectangle with cinnamon and sugar, then 1/3 cup raisins. Roll each rectangle up in jelly-roll fashion. Cut into slices 1-inch wide. Put each slice, cut side down, into a muffin cup. Cover and allow to rise in a warm place for 1 1/2 hours. Bake for 12 minutes or until golden brown. Cool rolls briefly in pan and then turn out immediately onto a board.

NUTRIENTS PER SERVING

126 calories, 5 gm. fat, 0 saturated fat, 8 mg. cholesterol with egg (0 with egg sub.), 35 mg. sodium, 20 gm. carbohydrate, 2 gm. protein

Count as 1 bread/starch and 1 fat for food exchange eating plans.

45 minutes "hands-on" preparation time, 12 hours dough resting time, 1 1/2 hours dough rising time, 12 minutes baking time

ZIGGY'S CHALLAH
ONLY 1 GRAM OF FAT

This recipe is shared by Paul Zhiss.
Serves 48, 1 slice each

2 pkg. dry yeast
1/2 cup lukewarm water
2 cups boiling water
3 Tbsp. vegetable oil
1 Tbsp. salt
1 Tbsp. sugar

2 eggs, well beaten or 1/2 cup liquid egg substitute
8 cups flour
Flour to coat work surface
1 egg

Soften yeast in lukewarm water. In a large mixing bowl, combine boiling water, oil, salt, and sugar. Stir until sugar is dissolved. When mixture has cooled to lukewarm, add softened yeast. Add beaten eggs. Stir in 3 cups of flour, beating until smooth. Allow dough to rest for 10 minutes. Add remaining flour and turn dough out onto a floured board. Knead dough until it is smooth and elastic. Allow dough to rise until double in bulk. Knead again until dough is fine grained. Divide dough in half, then cut each half into

3 pieces. Roll each piece into a long roll. Braid three strips together. Place braided dough on a baking sheet that has been sprayed with nonstick cooking spray. Allow dough to rise 1 hour. Preheat oven to 350° F. Beat 1 egg with 1 tsp. cold water. Brush surface of dough with egg and water mixture, then bake for 25 minutes until golden brown.

NUTRIENTS PER SERVING

144 calories, 1 gm. fat, 0 saturated fat, 9 mg. cholesterol with egg
(1 mg. with egg sub.), 102 mg. sodium, 30 gm. carbohydrate, 3 gm. protein

Count as 2 bread/starch for food exchange eating plans.

45 minutes "hands-on" preparation time, 2 hours initial rising time,
1 hour second rising time, 25 minutes baking time

COLUMBUS DAY

Significant Symbols

SHIPS

October 12 is the anniversary of the landing of Christopher Columbus in the New World. The historic event happened before dawn in 1492 when the lookout on the ship, the Pinta, shouted "Tierra! Tierra!" The holiday is celebrated in the United States as well as in Italy, where Columbus was born, and in Spain, where he sailed from.

ADD FUN, SUBTRACT EXPENSE

◆ *Fly the Italian flag together with the American Flag.*

◆ *Don't feel like cooking? Visit an Italian restaurant for ravioli or manicotti.*

◆ *Use three tiny ships in your centerpiece.*

MENU IDEAS

Christopher's Antipasto

Minestrone with Thin Bread Sticks

Garbanzo Bean Salad

Yogurt Pistachio Freeze

CHRISTOPHER'S ANTIPASTO

The term antipasto means "before the meal," and is an assortment of cold appetizers, artfully arranged on a glass serving tray.

Serves 8

1 lb. asparagus spears, cleaned, trimmed, and cut into 3-inch pieces

1/2 cup reduced-fat Italian dressing

8 oz. lean salami, sliced thin

8 oz. provolone cheese, sliced thin

3-oz. jar artichoke hearts, drained

3-oz. hot pickled peppers

Steam asparagus spears with 2 Tbsp. water in a covered baking dish for 3 minutes. Drain, then toss asparagus with 4 ice cubes to stop the cooking process, and drain again. Combine asparagus with Italian dressing and allow to marinate for at least 10 minutes. Meanwhile, arrange meat, cheese, artichoke hearts, and peppers on a glass serving tray. Place marinated asparagus on the tray, and serve.

NUTRIENTS PER SERVING

190 calories, 13 gm. fat, 5 gm. saturated fat, 43 mg. cholesterol, 649 mg. sodium, 5 gm. carbohydrate, 14 gm. protein

Count as 1 1/2 lean meat, 1 vegetable, and 2 fat for food exchange eating plans.

15 minutes "hands-on" preparation time

MINESTRONE WITH THIN BREAD STICKS

Serves 8, 1 1/2 cups each

1 lb. lean round steak,
 cut in 1/2-inch cubes
1 Tbsp. vegetable oil
1 large onion, peeled and sliced
1/4 tsp. minced garlic
4 cup no-added-salt beef broth
16-oz. can chunky tomatoes

1 tsp. oregano
1/2 tsp. thyme
1/2 tsp. pepper
1/2 cup white rice
1/2 lb. shredded cabbage
GARNISH: freshly grated
 Parmesan cheese

Heat oil in a large stockpot, and add cubes of round steak. Add onion and garlic. Cook until vegetables are tender. Add all remaining ingredients. Cook for 30 minutes or until rice and cabbage are tender. Ladle soup into bowls. If desired, garnish with freshly grated Parmesan cheese.

NUTRIENTS PER SERVING

*207 calories, 6 gm. fat, 1 gm. saturated fat, 43 mg. cholesterol,
775 mg. sodium (to reduce sodium, use no-added salt tomatoes),
16 gm. carbohydrate, 19 gm. protein*

*Count as 2 lean meat, 1 bread/starch, and 1 vegetable
for food exchange eating plans.*

15 minutes "hands-on" preparation time, 30 minutes cooking time

GARBANZO BEAN SALAD

ONLY 2 GRAMS OF FAT

Serves 8, 1/2 cup each

15-oz. can garbanzo beans, drained

1/4 tsp. garlic powder

1 tsp. vegetable oil

2 Tbsp. vinegar

2 stalks celery, finely chopped

1/2 cup sliced pitted green olives

1/4 cup chopped pimientos

4 green onions, diced

1/2 tsp. salt

1/8 tsp. black pepper

Combine all ingredients in a large salad bowl. Mix well and refrigerate for at least 30 minutes or up to 24 hours before serving. Serve salad on a spinach or romaine lettuce liner.

NUTRIENTS PER SERVING

79 calories, 2 gm. fat, 0 saturated fat, 0 cholesterol, 535 mg. sodium, 11 gm. carbohydrate, 3 gm. protein

Count as 1 bread/starch for food exchange eating plans.

15 minutes "hands-on" preparation time, 30 minutes chilling time

YOGURT PISTACHIO FREEZE

Serves 16, 1 slice each

3 cups vanilla frozen yogurt, softened

2 cups raspberry sherbet, softened

1 cup pistachio ice cream, softened

1/4 cup diced dried fruit (try any combination of apples, pears, apricots, papaya, pineapple, raisins, and dates)

2 Tbsp. rum

3 large egg whites

1/3 cup sugar

1 cup reduced fat whipped topping

OPTIONAL GARNISH: diced dried fruit

Line a 3-quart mold evenly with the vanilla frozen yogurt. Freeze until firm. Cover the frozen yogurt with a layer of raspberry sherbet, and freeze again. Then cover with a layer of pistachio ice cream and freeze again. Stir diced dried fruit and rum together in a small bowl. In a medium mixing bowl, beat the egg whites until foamy. Slowly beat in the sugar. Fold dried fruit and rum mixture slowly into the meringue. Fold whipped topping into the meringue. Spoon the meringue over the molded ice cream. Use a spatula to smooth the surface. Freeze until firm. To unmold, dip the outside of the mold in hot water for 6 seconds, and invert onto a cold platter. Slice into 16 servings. Garnish with additional chopped dried fruit.

NUTRIENTS PER SERVING

215 calories, 7 gm. fat, 4 gm. saturated fat, 6 mg. cholesterol, 76 mg. sodium, 34 gm. carbohydrate, 3 gm. protein

Count as 1 fruit, 1 bread/starch, and 1 1/2 fat for food exchange eating plans.

15 minutes "hands-on" preparation time, 45 minutes freezing time

HALLOWEEN

Significant Symbols

GHOSTS AND GOBLINS

Gaelic custom called for an autumn festival on the last day of October to mark the beginning of winter. Giant bonfires were symbolic ways to honor the sun god and to frighten away evil spirits. People danced and sang around the fires, pretending to be chased by evil spirits. It was also believed that witches rode through the skies on broomsticks, and on the night of the full moon, ghosts played tricks on humans and caused supernatural happenings. Even with its pagan roots, Halloween has become a widely celebrated American holiday.

JACK-O'-LANTERNS

The custom of orange carved faces began in the early United States after a plentiful fall harvest of pumpkins. Taffy pulls, corn-popping parties, and hayrides became part of the celebration.

COSTUMES

Simple white bed sheets were used for early costumes as revelers took on the part of trick and treating ghosts.

ADD FUN, SUBTRACT EXPENSE

 ◆ *Invite friends and family to an old-fashioned scavenger hunt. Assign teams to go around the neighborhood looking for common items such as an acorn, a feather, a thimble, a mini-pumpkin, an ear of Indian corn, etc.*

◆ Start early in the month and let the kids design their own simple costume to make. Instead of buying masks, let the kids paint their faces with face crayons.

◆ "Hide-and-seek" is especially scary on Halloween night. Provide flashlights for participants.

Chocolate candy bars are expensive and full of saturated fat. Consider giving your trick or treaters a choice of small boxes or packets of nuts, raisins, or dried fruit, single-serve cartons of 100% fruit juice, sticks of sugarless gum, single-serve boxes of dry cereal, packaged fruit rolls, single-serve packets of microwave popcorn, or commercially baked and wrapped muffins.

MENU IDEAS

COSTUME PARTY CHOW

Serve one of these in a pumpkin shell!
Picante Beef Stew or
Spicy Pumpkin Stew or
Calico Chili

Pumpkin Poppy Seed Cake

Quick Supper Before the Tricks Start

Veggie Omelet in a Cup

PICANTE BEEF STEW

Serves 8, 1 cup each

1 Tbsp. vegetable oil

1 lb. beef stew meat, cut into 1-inch cubes

1 large onion, chopped

1/4 tsp. garlic

14-oz. can no-added-salt beef broth

1/2 cup picante sauce or chunky salsa

1 medium zucchini, thinly sliced

2 tsp. cornstarch dissolved in 2 Tbsp. water

1 small tomato, peeled and cut into 8 wedges

Prepared pumpkin shell

In a Dutch oven, heat oil over medium heat until hot. Add beef, onions, and garlic and cook until onions are tender. Add all remaining ingredients. Simmer for 20 minutes.

To prepare pumpkin shell, cut top off a 5 lb. pumpkin. Scrape out fibers and seeds, and discard. Fill pumpkin shell at least three-quarters full with boiling water. Cover and let stand 10 minutes. Remove water before filling with stew.

NUTRIENTS PER SERVING

146 calories, 6 gm. fat, 1 gm. saturated fat, 43 mg. cholesterol, 470 mg. sodium, 6 gm. carbohydrate, 17 gm. protein

Count as 2 lean meat and 1 vegetable for food exchange eating plans.

10 minutes "hands-on" preparation time, 20 minutes simmering time

SPICY PUMPKIN STEW

ONLY 3 GRAMS OF FAT

Serves 8, 1 cup each

1 large yellow onion, chopped

1 large carrot, sliced thin

1 whole chicken breast, boned, skinned, and cut into 1-inch pieces

1 Tbsp. vegetable oil

3 large stalks celery, chopped

1 red bell pepper, diced

16-oz. can solid pack pumpkin

14-oz. can no-added-salt chicken broth

1/2 cup nonfat sour cream

15-oz. can hominy

3 Tbsp. chopped cilantro

1/2 tsp. salt

1/2 tsp. black pepper

1/2 tsp. oregano

1/2 tsp. cumin

1/8 tsp. nutmeg

Prepared pumpkin shell

In a large stockpot, sauté onion, carrot, and chicken in vegetable oil until chicken is no longer pink. Add celery and red pepper, and sauté for 4 more minutes. Stir in pumpkin, broth, sour cream, hominy, cilantro, salt, pepper, oregano, cumin, and nutmeg, and simmer over very low heat for 10 minutes or until heated through.

To prepare pumpkin shell, cut top off a 5 lb. pumpkin. Scrape out fibers and seeds, and discard. Fill pumpkin shell at least three-quarters full with boiling water. Cover and let stand 10 minutes. Remove water before filling with stew.

NUTRIENTS PER SERVING

147 calories, 3 gm. fat, 1 gm. saturated fat, 18 mg. cholesterol, 315 mg. sodium, 20 gm. carbohydrate, 37 gm. protein

Count as 1 bread/starch, 1 lean meat, and 1 vegetable for food exchange eating plans.

15 minutes "hands-on" preparation time, 10 minutes simmering time

CALICO CHILI

Serves 8, 1 1/4 cups each

1 lb. lean ground beef
1 large carrot, chopped
1 green pepper, chopped
1 yellow onion, chopped
2 stalks celery, chopped
3/4 tsp. minced garlic
2 16-oz. cans chunky tomatoes

16-oz. can dark red kidney beans, drained
2 Tbsp. chili powder
1 tsp. pepper
1 tsp. oregano
Prepared pumpkin shell

In a large stockpot, brown ground beef with carrots, pepper, onion, celery, and garlic. When beef is cooked through, drain mixture in a colander. Return beef and vegetables to the stockpot, then add all remaining ingredients, and simmer for 20 minutes.

To prepare pumpkin shell, cut top off a 5 lb. pumpkin. Scrape out fibers and seeds and discard. Fill pumpkin shell at least three-quarters full with boiling water. Cover and let stand 10 minutes. Remove water before filling with chili.

NUTRIENTS PER SERVING

239 calories, 9 gm. fat, 3 gm. saturated fat, 46 mg. cholesterol, 443 mg. sodium, 19 gm. carbohydrate, 18 gm. protein

Count as 2 lean meat, 1 bread/starch, and 2 vegetable for food exchange eating plans.

15 minutes "hands-on" preparation time, 30 minutes cooking time

PUMPKIN POPPY SEED CAKE

ONLY 3 GRAMS OF FAT

Serves 16

1 94% fat-free yellow
  cake mix

1 1/4 cups solid pack pumpkin

2/3 cup orange juice

3 eggs

2 Tbsp. poppy seeds

2 Tbsp. finely grated orange rind

Preheat oven to 350° F. Combine cake mix, pumpkin, orange juice, and eggs in a large mixing bowl. Beat at low speed for 30 seconds. Beat at medium speed for 3 more minutes. Fold in poppy seeds and orange rind. Pour into a Bundt pan that has been sprayed with nonstick cooking spray. Bake for 35 minutes. Cool for 10 minutes, then invert onto a wire rack to cool completely. Serve with orange or lemon sherbet.

NUTRIENTS PER SERVING

*153 calories, 3 gm. fat, 0 saturated fat, 40 mg. cholesterol,
245 mg. sodium, 29 gm. carbohydrate, 4 gm. protein*

Count as 2 bread/starch for food exchange eating plans.

15 minutes "hands-on" preparation time, 35 minutes baking time

VEGGIE OMELET IN A CUP

Serves 8

8 strips bacon, finely diced

1 large carrot, cleaned, peeled, and shredded

1 large stalk broccoli, chopped fine

1 green onion, chopped

12 eggs or 3 cups liquid egg substitute

1/4 cup milk

2 oz. reduced-fat cheddar cheese, shredded

Preheat oven to 400° F. Cook bacon in a medium skillet over medium heat until crisp. Drain well and set aside. Prepare vegetables. Beat eggs and milk in a large mixing bowl until foamy. Fold in prepared vegetables, bacon, and cheese. Pour into 8 ramekins (oven-proof soup or large custard cups) that have been sprayed with nonstick cooking spray. Bake for 20 minutes or until puffed up and golden brown.

NUTRIENTS PER SERVING

189 calories, 12 gm. fat, 4 gm. saturated fat, 329 mg. cholesterol with egg (11 mg. with egg sub.), 269 mg. sodium, 5 gm. carbohydrate, 15 gm. protein

Count as 2 lean meat, 1 fat (1/2 fat with egg substitute), and 1 vegetable for food exchange eating plans.

15 minutes "hands-on" preparation time, 20 minutes baking time

Significant Symbols

DONKEYS AND ELEPHANTS

In 1845, Congress set the first Tuesday after the first Monday in November as the day for presidential elections. Donkeys represent the Democratic party and elephants represent the Republican party.

ADD FUN, SUBTRACT EXPENSE

◆ *Ask everyone in the family to cast a mock ballot predicting the winners of interesting races. Open the ballots after the returns come in to see who won.*

◆ *Adults and kids alike love to debate. Let the children take turns being the candidates, and discuss election issues at the dinner table.*

MENU IDEAS

COFFEE AND CANDIDATE CHATTER

Caramel Rolls or
Amy's Brownies

WATCH THE RETURNS NIBBLES

Slow-Cook Pork and Vegetable Stew or
Round Steak Pot Pie

Marinated Radishes, Baby Carrots, and Peppers

Harvest Compote with Ice Milk

CARAMEL ROLLS

Serves 24

1 1/4 cups sifted powdered sugar
1/2 cup evaporated skim milk
1/2 cup chopped pecans
2 1-lb. loaves sweet bread dough, thawed

3 Tbsp. soft margarine, melted
1/2 cup packed brown sugar
1 Tbsp. ground cinnamon
1/2 cup chopped raisins

To prepare caramel topping: mix powdered sugar with evaporated skim milk in a small mixing bowl. Spread half of mixture in each of two 9-inch round baking pans. Sprinkle chopped pecans evenly over mixture.

On a lightly floured board, roll each loaf of dough into a 12- by 8-inch rectangle. Brush with melted margarine. In a small mixing bowl, stir together brown sugar and cinnamon, and sprinkle over the dough. Top with chopped raisins. Roll up rectangles, jelly-roll style, starting from the long side. Pinch the edges to seal and cut each one into 12 slices. Place rolls, cut side down, on top of sugar mixture. Allow rolls to rise in a warm place until nearly double (about 30 minutes), or the rolls can be covered and held in the refrigerator for up to 24 hours. Bake the rolls in a 375° F oven, about 25 minutes or until golden brown. Cool in the pans for 5 minutes on a wire rack, then invert onto a serving plate. These rolls are best when served warm. The second plate of rolls can be cooled, covered, and frozen for future use. To rewarm, thaw to room temperature, then microcook for 90 seconds on 50-percent power.

NUTRIENTS PER SERVING

206 calories, 6 gm. fat, 1 gm. saturated fat, 0 cholesterol, 301 mg. sodium, 33 gm. carbohydrate, 5 gm. protein

Count as 2 bread/starch and 1 fat for food exchange eating plans.

20 minutes "hands-on" preparation time, 30 minutes rising time, 25 minutes baking time

AMY'S BROWNIES

ONLY 1 GRAM OF FAT

A recipe shared with my Sarah Circle by Amy Farlinger.
Some of the original "sins" have been removed.
Serves 36

15 caramels	1/4 cup margarine, melted
1/2 cup evaporated skim milk	2/3 cup evaporated skim milk
18-oz. pkg. German chocolate cake mix	1/2 cup mini chocolate chips

Preheat oven to 350° F. Melt together and stir constantly the caramels and 1/2 cup milk. Set aside. In a large mixing bowl, stir by hand the cake mix, melted margarine and 2/3 cup evaporated milk. Press half of the cake mixture in the bottom of a 9- by 13-inch cake pan that has been sprayed with nonstick cooking spray. Bake for 6 minutes. Remove from oven and sprinkle with chocolate chips. Then drizzle caramel mixture on top. Crumble remaining cake mixture on top. Bake for 15 more minutes. Cool. Cut into 36 squares and refrigerate.

Nutrients per serving

82 calories, 1 gm. fat, 0 saturated fat, 0 cholesterol, 117 mg. sodium, 16 gm. carbohydrate, 1 gm. protein

Count as 1 bread/starch for food exchange eating plans.

15 minutes "hands-on" preparation time, 20 minutes baking time

SLOW-COOK PORK AND VEGETABLE STEW

Serves 8, 1/2 cup each

1 1/2 lb. boneless lean pork loin, cut in 3/4-inch cubes

1 tsp. vegetable oil

2 14-oz. can stewed tomatoes

1/4 cup red wine

1 tsp. basil

1/2 tsp. oregano

1/4 tsp. black pepper

1/8 tsp. ground red pepper

3 medium carrots, cut in 1/2-inch slices

1 cup frozen pearl onions

9-oz. Italian green beans

2 Tbsp. cornstarch

2 Tbsp. water

In a large Dutch oven or deep skillet with lid, brown pork in oil over medium heat until browned. Add tomatoes, wine, seasonings, and vegetables. Cover and simmer over medium-low heat for 20 minutes. Combine cornstarch and water in a small cup and stir into the hot mixture. Simmer until thickened, about 5 more minutes.

NUTRIENTS PER SERVING

236 calories, 8 gm. fat, 4 gm. saturated fat, 82 mg. cholesterol, 318 mg. sodium, 15 gm. carbohydrate, 26 gm. protein

Count as 3 lean meat and 3 vegetable for food exchange eating plans.

20 minutes "hands-on" preparation time, 25 minutes cooking time

ROUND STEAK POT PIE

Serves 8

1 Tbsp vegetable oil

1 1/2 lb. boneless round steak, cut into 2-inch strips

3 Tbsp. flour

1 large yellow onion, thinly sliced

2 medium potatoes, peeled and cut into bite-size chunks

1 medium carrot, thinly sliced

1 cup beer

1/2 cup no-added-salt beef broth

2 Tbsp. tomato paste

1 bay leaf

1/2 tsp. thyme, crushed

1/2 tsp. marjoram

1/2 tsp. minced garlic

2 Tbsp. flour

1/4 cup beer

2 tubes buttermilk biscuits

Preheat oven to 400° F. In a Dutch oven, heat vegetable oil over medium-high heat until hot. In a shallow dish, roll beef cubes in flour. Brown floured beef cubes in oil. Add onion, potatoes, carrot, beer, broth, tomato paste, and seasonings. Stir to mix and simmer for 10 minutes. In a small cup, combine flour and 1/4 cup beer. Stir into beef and vegetable mixture, and cook until thick. Meanwhile, remove biscuits from tubes. Spray a 9-inch pie pan with nonstick cooking spray. Arrange 1 1/2 tubes of biscuits on the bottom and up the sides of the pan. Flatten the biscuits to cover the entire surface area. Pour beef mixture into the biscuit-lined pan. Place remaining 1/2 tube of biscuits over the top. Bake for 20 minutes or until biscuits are browned on top.

NUTRIENTS PER SERVING

333 calories, 10 gm. fat, 3 gm. saturated fat, 65 mg. cholesterol, 447 mg. sodium, 33 gm. carbohydrate, 28 gm. protein

Count as 3 lean meat and 2 bread/starch for food exchange eating plans

20 minutes "hands-on" preparation time, 15 minutes cooking time, 20 minutes baking time

MARINATED RADISHES, BABY CARROTS, AND PEPPERS

ONLY 1 GRAM OF FAT

Serves 8, 1 cup each

1 lb. bag baby carrots, washed

1 Tbsp. water

8-oz. bag radishes, cleaned and sliced thin

1 large green pepper, finely diced

1 pkg. dry Italian dressing mix

1/4 cup red wine

1 Tbsp. oil

1/4 cup vinegar

1 Tbsp. water

1/2 tsp. fennel

Combine carrots and water in a microwave-safe casserole dish. Cover and microwave on high power for 3 minutes. Remove from oven, and cover with 3 large ice cubes. Meanwhile, combine sliced radishes and diced pepper in a salad bowl. In a shaker container, combine dressing mix with remaining ingredients. Shake well. Drain carrots and add to salad bowl. Pour dressing over vegetables, stir to mix, then cover and marinate in the refrigerator for at least 30 minutes or up to 2 days. Drain marinade before serving as a vegetable salad.

NUTRIENTS PER SERVING

53 calories, 1 gm. fat, 0 saturated fat, 0 cholesterol, 139 mg. sodium, 8 gm. carbohydrate, 0 protein

Count as 2 vegetable for food exchange eating plans.

15 minutes "hands-on" preparation time, 30 minutes marinating time

HARVEST COMPOTE WITH ICE MILK

Serves 8, 1/2 cup each +
1/2 cup ice milk

1 orange

1 cup water

1/4 cup sugar

2 3-inch cinnamon sticks

1 pear

1 Granny Smith apple

1/2 cup mixed dried fruit, diced
(choose from papaya, dates,
raisins, apricots)

4 cups ice milk

With a sharp knife, remove a thin 4-inch strip of peel from orange. Squeeze juice from orange into a large saucepan; add 1 cup water, orange peel, sugar, and cinnamon sticks. Bring to a boil. Meanwhile peel and core pear and apple; cut into eighths. Add pear and apple slices to the saucepan, then return to boil over medium heat. Add dried fruit, and cook covered over low heat for 5 minutes or until pears are barely tender. Let stand, covered for 10 minutes. Serve hot over ice milk.

NUTRIENTS PER SERVING

214 calories, 5 gm. fat, 3 gm. saturated fat, 15 mg. cholesterol,
98 mg. sodium, 40 gm. carbohydrate, 5 gm. protein

Count as 1/2 skim milk, 2 fruit, and 1 fat for food exchange eating plans.

15 minutes "hands-on" preparation time, 15 minutes cooking time

Significant Symbols

FLAGS AND PARADES

November 11 is the anniversary of the signing of the Armistice by
the Allies and Germans ending World War I. A legal holiday in
all states, the day is marked with parades honoring all veterans.

ADD FUN, SUBTRACT EXPENSE

◆ *If the kids are out of school for the day, visit a local war
   monument, museum, or art gallery.*

◆ *Visit with friends and family who served our country to
   learn more about their contribution.*

◆ *Rent an old movie about World War I.*

MENU IDEAS

AFTER THE PARADE LUNCHEON

Oven Fried Chicken

Zesty Pork and Beans

Fresh Vegetable Relishes

Coconut Cream Dessert Pizza

OVEN FRIED CHICKEN

Serves 8

1 1/2 cups nonfat plain yogurt

1 1/2 tsp. paprika

1 1/2 tsp. thyme

1/2 tsp. garlic powder

1/4 tsp. salt

1/4 tsp. cayenne pepper

8 boneless skinned chicken breast halves

1 1/2 cups finely crushed bread crumbs

1 1/2 Tbsp. margarine, melted

Preheat oven to 400° F. Combine yogurt, paprika, thyme, garlic powder, salt, and pepper in a shallow bowl. Coat chicken with this mixture. In another shallow bowl, combine bread crumbs with melted margarine. Roll chicken breasts in bread crumbs. Place on a baking sheet that has been sprayed with nonstick cooking spray. Bake for 25 minutes.

NUTRIENTS PER SERVING

244 calories, 8 gm. fat, 2 gm. saturated fat, 69 mg. cholesterol, 424 mg. sodium, 17 gm. carbohydrate, 26 gm. protein

Count as 3 lean meat and 1 bread/starch for food exchange eating plans.

15 minutes "hands-on" preparation time, 25 minutes baking time

ZESTY PORK AND BEANS

FAT-FREE!

Serves 8, 3/4 cup each

15-oz. can kidney beans, drained   8-oz. jar thick and chunky salsa
22-oz. can pork and beans

Preheat oven to 400° F. Combine beans with salsa in a 2-quart casserole dish. Bake for 30 minutes until bubbly.

NUTRIENTS PER SERVING

*124 calories, 0 fat, 0 saturated fat, 0 cholesterol, 847 mg. sodium
(to reduce sodium, use 8 oz. no-added-salt chunky tomatoes and 1 Tbsp.
Mexican seasoning instead of salsa), 23 gm. carbohydrate, 6 gm. protein*

Count as 1 1/2 bread/starch for food exchange eating plans.

5 minutes "hands-on" preparation time, 30 minutes baking time

COCONUT CREAM DESSERT PIZZA

*This recipe comes from a former student
and now fellow registered dietitian, Vicki Heiller.*
Serves 16

1 loaf frozen bread dough

8 oz. reduced-fat cream cheese,
  softened to room temperature

1/3 cup sugar

1 egg

1 tsp. almond extract

TOPPING:

1/2 cup sugar

1/4 cup margarine, melted

2/3 cup flour

1/4 cup sliced almonds

1/4 cup flaked coconut

Thaw bread and press into a 12-inch round pizza pan that has been sprayed with nonstick cooking spray. In a small bowl, combine softened cream cheese, sugar, egg, and almond extract. Spread over dough. Mix together ingredients for topping. Crumble on cream cheese mixture. Bake for 25 minutes. Sprinkle with powdered sugar and transfer to a large glass dessert plate for serving.

NUTRIENTS PER SERVING

216 calories, 8 gm. fat, 3 gm. saturated fat, 18 mg. cholesterol, 322 mg. sodium, 30 gm. carbohydrate, 6 gm. protein

Count as 2 bread/starch and 1 fat for food exchange eating plans.

15 minutes "hands-on" preparation time, 25 minutes baking time

THANKSGIVING

Significant Symbols

PILGRIMS

One hundred two Pilgrims celebrated the first harvest in Plymouth, Massachusetts, after having crossed the Atlantic on the Mayflower in 1621.

TURKEY AND PUMPKIN

The pilgrims had a very different feast than we have today. Four men were sent "fowling" and they returned with a bunch of birds. In the language of the 17th century Pilgrims, turkey simply meant any bird with a featherless head, rounded body, and dark feathers. The menu of 300 years ago included watercress plucked from the clear streams, leeks, bitter wild plums, dried berries, fried corn cakes, wild cranberries and boiled pumpkin. (The Pilgrims' flour supply had been exhausted, and thus there was no pie at the first Thanksgiving.)

INDIANS

Native Americans were important partners in the first Thanksgiving. Share their respect for creation by spending part of Thanksgiving weekend outdoors!

ADD FUN, SUBTRACT EXPENSE

◆ *Place a cornucopia or "horn of plenty" on your table and invite family members to fill it with items that represent how they have been blessed. Include foods and symbols of personal blessing such as photos.*

◆ At the conclusion of the Thanksgiving meal, set a "blessing basket" in the middle of the table. From that day until Christmas, add food and gifts to the basket each day for a needy family.

◆ Follow the example the Pilgrims set by reflecting on the Bible and spiritual needs before mealtime.

◆ Use Thanksgiving weekend to design a plan for your family Christmas celebration. Allow all members to submit items to the list such as "Favorite Christmas Cookie," "Favorite Christmas Party," "Favorite Decoration," and "Wish List for the Perfect Gift." Continue the plan with a schedule of who, how, and when the items will be accomplished.

MENU IDEAS

Roast Turkey with Spicy Orange Sauce or
Maple Glaze

Zucchini Dressing

John's Crunchy Cranberry Relish or
Cran-Apple Mold

Green Bean and Wild Rice Casserole

CHOOSE A PUMPKIN DESSERT

Low-Fat Pumpkin Pie #1

Low-Fat Pumpkin Pie # 2

No-Bake Pumpkin Cheesecake

Honey of a Pumpkin Bread

WEEKEND AFTER TURKEY MAKEOVERS

Turkey and Vegetable Bake or
Use-It-Up Turkey Casserole

White Bean and Endive Salad

Crunchy Apple Quick Bread

Roast Turkey

Tips on turning out a perfect bird

Purchase:

Allow 3/4 to 1 lb. of turkey per person to be served. This method ensures plenty of white and dark meat to suit individual taste and allows for some leftovers.

Preparation for roasting:

Thaw a frozen turkey, breast side up, in its unopened wrapper on a tray in the refrigerator. Estimate at least one day of thawing for every 6 pounds of turkey. Do not thaw at room temperature. Remove original plastic wrapper from thawed or fresh turkey, then remove neck and giblets from the body cavity. Rinse the turkey inside and out with cool water, and pat dry with paper towels. Stuff turkey lightly if desired. Return legs to tuck position, if untucked. Insert a meat thermometer into the deepest part of the thigh. Place turkey, breast up, on a flat rack in a shallow pan. Brush skin with vegetable oil. Place in preheated 325° F oven. When skin is golden brown, shield the breast loosely with a tent of foil to prevent overbrowning. Roast to an internal temperature of 180° in the thigh, 170° in the breast, and 160° in the stuffing. Begin checking for doneness 30 minutes before anticipated end of cooking.

GUIDELINES FOR ESTIMATING COOKING TIME:

WEIGHT OF TURKEY	COOKING TIME IN HOURS	
	STUFFED	UNSTUFFED
10 to 18 lb.	4 to 4/12	3 to 3 1/2
18 to 22 lb.	4 1/2 to 5	3 1/2 to 4
22 to 24 lb.	5 to 5 1/2	4 to 4 1/2
24 to 29 lb.	5 1/2 to 6 1/2	4 1/2 to 5

When appropriate temperature has been attained, remove turkey from the oven, cover, and allow to rest at room temperature 20 to 30 minutes before carving.

NUTRIENTS PER 4 OZ. SERVING OF ROAST TURKEY WITHOUT SKIN

193 calories, 6 gm. fat, 2 gm. saturated fat, 86 mg. cholesterol, 79 mg. sodium, 0 carbohydrate, 33 gm. protein

Count as 3 1/2 lean meat for food exchange eating plans.

15 minutes "hands-on" preparation time, see chart for roasting time

SPICY ORANGE GLAZE
FAT-FREE!

Glazes a 12 to 18 lb. turkey.
24 servings, 1 1/2 Tbsp. each

1 1/2 cups orange marmalade   2 tsp. prepared horseradish
1/3 cup white wine   1 Tbsp. dried onion
1 Tbsp. Dijon-style mustard

Combine ingredients for glaze. Use a spoon or pastry brush to spread glaze over turkey during final 30 minutes of roasting.

If the turkey is to be sliced and served on a platter, I recommend heating the glaze to steaming, then pouring over the sliced meat and/or passing glaze at the table for individual service.

NUTRIENTS PER SERVING

48 calories, 0 fat, 0 saturated fat, 0 cholesterol,
17 mg. sodium, 12 gm. carbohydrate, 0 protein

Count as 1/2 fruit for food exchange eating plans.

10 minutes "hands-on" preparation time

MAPLE GLAZE

FAT-FREE!

Glazes a 12 to 18 lb. turkey.
24 servings, 1 1/2 Tbsp. each

1 large yellow onion, finely chopped

2 stalks celery, including tops, finely diced

1 large golden Delicious apple, shredded

1/4 tsp. salt

1/2 tsp. black pepper

1/4 tsp. dry mustard

1/4 tsp. sage

1 cup maple syrup

Combine all ingredients in a saucepan. Simmer uncovered for 30 minutes. Use a spoon or pastry brush to spread glaze over turkey during final 30 minutes of roasting.

If the turkey is to be sliced and served on a platter, I recommend heating the glaze to steaming, then pouring over the sliced meat and/or passing glaze at the table for individual service.

NUTRIENTS PER SERVING

40 calories, 0 fat, 0 saturated fat, 0 cholesterol,
26 mg. sodium, 10 gm. carbohydrate, 0 protein

Count as 1/2 fruit for food exchange eating plans.

15 minutes "hands-on" preparation time

ZUCCHINI DRESSING

ONLY 2 GRAMS OF FAT

Serves 8, 1 cup each

4 medium zucchini, peeled and diced

1 large onion, chopped

1 red pepper, chopped

1/4 cup fresh parsley, minced

1 tsp. salt

1/4 tsp. cayenne

1/8 tsp. black pepper

2 tsp. sage

1/2 tsp. minced garlic

2 cups no-added-salt chicken broth

1-lb. bag dry croutons or bread crumbs

Preheat oven to 325 to 350° F. Combine all ingredients in a 3-quart baking dish that has been sprayed with nonstick cooking spray. Use as stuffing for the turkey or bake uncovered for 1 hour. If dressing starts to get dry, add additional fat-free chicken or turkey broth.

NUTRIENTS PER SERVING

142 calories, 2 gm. fat, 0 saturated fat, 0 cholesterol,
755 mg. sodium (to reduce sodium, reduce or omit salt),
26 gm. carbohydrate, 5 gm. protein

Count as 1 bread/starch and 2 vegetable for food exchange eating plans.

15 minutes "hands-on" preparation time, 1 hour baking time

JOHN'S CRUNCHY CRANBERRY RELISH

FAT-FREE!

A favorite of my favorite sibling, John Rewoldt.
Serves 8, 3/4 cup each

2 cups orange juice

2 3-oz. pkgs. raspberry gelatin

1-lb. bag cranberries

2 red Delicious apples, cored

2 stalks celery, diced

Heat 1 cup orange juice to boiling. In a large mixing bowl, combine raspberry gelatin with boiling juice. Stir to fully dissolve. Stir in remaining orange juice and refrigerate. Meanwhile, use a food grinder or food processor to finely mince cranberries and apples. Fold minced fruits into gelatin. Fold in celery, and transfer mixture to a pretty crystal or clear glass serving bowl, using a spatula to smooth out top of salad. Refrigerate for at least 3 hours. This salad is a great keeper.

NUTRIENTS PER SERVING

109 calories, 0 fat, 0 saturated fat, 0 cholesterol,
48 mg. sodium, 26 gm. carbohydrate, 1 gm. protein

Count as 2 fruit for food exchange eating plans.

20 minutes "hands-on" preparation time, 3 hours chilling time

CRAN-APPLE MOLD

FAT-FREE!

Serves 12, 1/2 cup each

1 1/2 cups boiling water

2 3-oz. pkgs. cranberry flavored gelatin (may substitute any red flavor)

16-oz. can whole berry cranberry sauce

1 cup cold water

1/2 tsp. ground cinnamon

1 medium apple, chopped

In a large bowl, stir boiling water into gelatin, and stir until completely dissolved. Stir in cranberry sauce, cold water, and cinnamon. Refrigerate about 1 1/2 hours or until thickened. Stir in apple and transfer to a 2 quart mold. Refrigerate at least 3 hours or until firm.

NUTRIENTS PER SERVING

109 calories, 0 fat, 0 saturated fat, 0 cholesterol, 36 mg. sodium, 27 gm. carbohydrate, 1 gm. protein

Count as 1 1/2 fruit for food exchange eating plans.

15 minutes "hands-on" preparation time, 3 hours chilling time

GREEN BEAN AND WILD RICE CASSEROLE

ONLY 2 GRAMS OF FAT

Serves 8, 1 cup each

1 cup wild rice
6 cups water
2 16-oz. pkgs. frozen French-cut green beans, thawed and drained

10-oz. can reduced fat cream of mushroom soup
3/4 cup skim milk
1/8 tsp. pepper
1/4 cup chopped pimiento

Preheat oven to 375° F. In a large saucepan, boil 6 cups of water and add wild rice. Combine thawed beans, soup, milk, pepper, and pimiento in a 3-quart baking dish that has been sprayed with non-stick cooking spray. When rice is cooked tender (at least 40 minutes), drain well, and fold into green bean mixture. Bake uncovered for 30 minutes.

NUTRIENTS PER SERVING

172 calories, 2 gm. fat, 0 saturated fat, 0 cholesterol, 241 mg. sodium, 29 gm. carbohydrate, 8 gm. protein

Count as 1 1/2 bread/starch and 2 vegetable for food exchange eating plans.

15 minutes "hands-on" preparation time, 40 minutes cooking time, 30 minutes baking time

LOW-FAT PUMPKIN PIE #1

Serves 12

9-inch prepared graham cracker crust

16-oz. can pumpkin

14-oz. can low-fat sweetened condensed milk

2 eggs or 1/2 cup liquid egg substitute

1 tsp. cinnamon

1/2 tsp. ginger

1/2 tsp. nutmeg

1/2 tsp. salt

Preheat oven to 425° F. In a large mixing bowl, beat pumpkin, milk, eggs and spices together until smooth. Pour into the crust, and bake for 15 minutes. Reduce oven temperature to 350° F. Bake for 40 minutes longer or until knife inserted 1 inch from the edge comes out clean. Cool and serve. Refrigerate leftovers.

NUTRIENTS PER SERVING

260 calories, 8 gm. fat, 2 gm. saturated fat, 76 mg. cholesterol with egg (12 mg. with egg sub.), 250 mg. sodium, 41 gm. carbohydrate, 6 gm. protein

Count as 2 bread/starch, 1 fruit, and 1 fat for food exchange eating plans.

10 minutes "hands-on" preparation time, 55 minutes baking time

••

LOW-FAT PUMPKIN PIE #2

Serves 12

9-inch prepared graham cracker crust

16-oz. can solid pack pumpkin

13-oz. can evaporated skim milk

2/3 cup packed brown sugar

3 eggs or 3/4 cup liquid egg substitute

1 tsp. pumpkin pie spice

1 tsp. vanilla

1/4 tsp salt

Preheat oven to 375° F. In a blender container or large mixing bowl, blend or beat pumpkin, milk, sugar, eggs, and spices until well blended. Pour into crust. Bake on bottom rack of oven until knife inserted 1 inch from the edge comes out clean, about 55 minutes. Cool on a wire rack.

NUTRIENTS PER SERVING

198 calories, 6 gm. fat, 1 gm. saturated fat, 53 mg. cholesterol with egg (1 mg. with egg sub.), 214 mg. sodium, 31 gm. carbohydrate, 5 gm. protein

Count as 1 bread/starch, 1 fruit, and 1 fat for food exchange eating plans.

10 minutes "hands-on" preparation time, 55 minutes baking time

NO-BAKE PUMPKIN CHEESECAKE

Serves 12

4 oz. reduced-fat cream cheese, softened

1 Tbsp. skim milk

1 Tbsp. sugar

1 1/2 cups reduced-fat whipped topping

9-inch prepared graham cracker crust

1 cup cold skim milk

2 3-oz. pkgs. vanilla flavor instant pudding and pie filling

16-oz. can solid pack pumpkin

1 tsp. cinnamon

1/2 tsp. ground ginger

1/4 tsp. ground cloves

Mix softened cream cheese, 1 tablespoon milk, and sugar in a large bowl with a wire whisk until smooth. Gently stir in whipped topping. Spread on the bottom of prepared crust. Pour 1 cup of milk into a bowl. Add pudding mixes, and beat with a wire whisk for 1 minute. Stir in pumpkin and spices, and spread over cream cheese layer. Refrigerate at least 3 hours or until set.

NUTRIENTS PER SERVING

267 calories, 11 gm. fat, 5 gm. saturated fat, 9 mg. cholesterol, 441 mg. sodium, 37 gm. carbohydrate, 5 gm. protein

Count as 1 fruit, 1 bread/starch, 1/2 skim milk, and 2 fat for food exchange eating plans.

15 minutes "hands-on" preparation time, 3 hours chilling time

HONEY OF A PUMPKIN BREAD

Serves 16

2 1/4 cups flour
3/4 cup wheat germ
2 1/2 tsp. baking powder
1 1/2 tsp. cinnamon
1 tsp. salt
1/2 tsp. baking soda
2 eggs or 1/2 cup liquid egg
   substitute

1 1/2 cups solid pack pumpkin
3/4 cup honey
3 Tbsp. oil
1/4 cup skim milk
1 Tbsp. sunflower seeds

Combine flour, wheat germ, baking powder, cinnamon, salt, and baking soda in a large mixing bowl. Combine eggs, pumpkin, honey, oil, and milk in medium bowl. Add to flour mixture, stirring just until blended. Spread batter into a loaf pan that has been sprayed with nonstick cooking spray. Sprinkle the top of the batter with sunflower seeds. Bake for 55 minutes or until a toothpick inserted in the center comes out clean. Cool in the pan for 10 minutes, then remove to a wire rack to cool. Makes 1 large loaf of approximately 16 slices.

NUTRIENTS PER SERVING

224 calories, 4 gm. fat, 0 saturated fat, 27 mg. cholesterol with egg (0 with egg sub.), 185 mg. sodium, 40 gm. carbohydrate, 7 gm. protein

Count as 2 bread/starch and 1 fruit for food exchange eating plans.

15 minutes "hands-on" preparation time, 55 minutes baking time

TURKEY AND VEGETABLE BAKE

Serves 8, 1 1/2 cups each

2 10-oz. cans reduced-fat cream
   of chicken soup
1 cup skim milk
20-oz. pkg. frozen California blend
   vegetables, thawed

1 small red pepper, diced
3 cups chopped cooked turkey
1 Tbsp. Worcestershire sauce

Preheat oven to 375° F. Combine all ingredients in a 3-quart casserole dish that has been sprayed with nonstick cooking spray. Bake uncovered for 45 minutes.

NUTRIENTS PER SERVING

*202 calories, 5 gm. fat, 1 gm. saturated fat, 62 mg. cholesterol,
481 mg. sodium, 8 gm. carbohydrate, 29 gm. protein*

Count as 3 lean meat and 2 vegetable for food exchange eating plans.

15 minutes "hands-on" preparation time, 45 minutes baking time

USE IT UP TURKEY CASSEROLE

Serves 8

1 cup diced cooked turkey

1 cup frozen peas and carrots

2 green onions, finely chopped

1 cup fresh cranberries or 1/2 cup cranberry relish

1 cup prepared turkey stuffing

3/4 cup reduced-fat baking mix (such as Bisquick® light)

1/4 tsp. salt

1 1/4 cups skim milk

3 eggs or 3/4 cup liquid egg substitute

Preheat oven to 400° F. Spray a 9-inch pie plate with nonstick cooking spray. Mix turkey, peas and carrots, onion, and cranberries in plate. Separate stuffing into small pieces on turkey mixture. Stir remaining ingredients in a medium bowl with a fork until blended. Pour into the pie plate. Bake for 30 minutes. Allow pie to sit at room temperature 5 minutes before slicing.

NUTRIENTS PER SERVING

228 calories, 7 gm. fat, 1 gm. saturated fat, 100 mg. cholesterol with egg (21 mg. with egg sub.), 509 mg. sodium, 24 gm. carbohydrate, 16 gm. protein

Count as 1 1/2 bread/starch and 2 lean meat for food exchange eating plans.

15 minutes "hands-on" preparation time, 30 minutes baking time

WHITE BEAN AND ENDIVE SALAD

This salad is good with cold turkey sandwiches.
Serves 8, 1 cup each

10-oz. pkg. frozen corn, thawed

1 red pepper, diced

2 16-oz. cans white beans, rinsed and drained

1 bunch green onions, trimmed and diced thin

1 head curly endive, torn into bite-size pieces

1/4 tsp. salt

1/2 tsp. black pepper

1/4 cup vinegar

2 Tbsp. lemon juice

2 Tbsp. Dijon-style mustard

2 Tbsp. vegetable oil

Combine corn, pepper, drained beans, chopped onions, and curly endive in a large salad bowl. In a shaker container, combine remaining ingredients. Shake well and pour over salad, tossing to coat vegetables. Chill until service.

NUTRIENTS PER SERVING

210 calories, 4 gm. fat, 0 saturated fat, 0 cholesterol,
144 mg. sodium, 35 gm. carbohydrate, 11 gm. protein

Count as 1 bread/starch, 1 lean meat, 2 vegetable,
and 1/2 fat for food exchange eating plans.

15 minutes "hands-on" preparation time

CRUNCHY APPLE QUICK BREAD

Serves 12, 1 slice each

8-oz. pkg. reduced-fat cream cheese, softened

2 Tbsp. sugar

1 egg or 1/4 cup liquid egg substitute

2 small tart apples, chopped fine

12-oz. pkg. apple, bran, pumpkin, or cranberry quick bread mix such as Pillsbury®

3/4 cup water

3 Tbsp. vegetable oil

1 egg or 1/4 cup liquid egg substitute

1 tsp. almond extract

1/4 cup apple jelly, melted

Preheat oven to 350° F. Spray a loaf pan with nonstick cooking spray. In a small bowl, blend softened cream cheese, sugar, 1 egg, and 1/2 of chopped apple. In a large bowl, combine quick bread mix, remaining apple, water, oil, egg, and almond extract. Stir with a spoon until dry ingredients are moist. Pour half of batter into the prepared pan. Carefully spoon cream cheese filling over the batter. Spoon remaining batter on top of filling. Spread with melted apple jelly. Bake for 70 minutes or until a toothpick inserted near the center of the bread comes out clean. Cool for 10 minutes on a wire rack, then remove from the pan.

NUTRIENTS PER SERVING

144 calories, 4 gm. fat, 0 saturated fat, 14 mg. cholesterol with egg (6 mg. with egg sub.), 24 mg. sodium, 22 gm. carbohydrate, 3 gm. protein

Count as 1 bread/starch and 1 fruit for food exchange eating plans.

20 minutes "hands-on" preparation time, 70 minutes baking time, 10 minutes cooling time

Significant Symbols

LIGHTS

Hanukkah is an eight-day Jewish "Festival of Lights" that begins in late November or early December and has been mistakenly linked to Christmas. The celebration of religious freedom, thought to have originated in 165 B.C., is symbolized by lighting a menorah, a nine-branched candelabrum. The legend of the light says that after a war victory, the Jewish Maccabees noticed that the eternal light over the altar had only enough pure oil to burn for one day. By a miracle, the oil lasted for eight days until new oil could be prepared. Because of the miracle of the oil, traditional foods for Hanukkah, such as potato kneidel, are cooked in oil.

GIFTS

Simple gifts are exchanged among family and friends—candy, cakes, and money.

MENU IDEAS

Vegetarian Tzimmes

Potato Kneidel

Chocolate Almond Macaroons

VEGETARIAN TZIMMES

ONLY 1 GRAM OF FAT

Thank you, Julia Cushman.
Serves 12, 1 cup each

1 lb. carrots	2 medium white potatoes
1 Tbsp. vegetable broth powder	1 cup dried apricots
1 1/2 cups water	1 cup brown sugar
3 Tbsp. soft reduced-fat margarine	1/2 tsp. salt
5 medium sweet potatoes	1/2 tsp. pepper

Clean carrots and cut into 1-inch slices. Place in a Dutch oven with vegetable broth powder, water, and margarine. Simmer over medium heat for 10 minutes. Meanwhile, cut sweet potatoes into 1 1/2-inch chunks, add to the Dutch oven, and continue simmering. While carrots and sweet potatoes are cooking, peel white potatoes and cut into 1 1/2-inch chunks, and add to the pot along with dried apricots. Continue to simmer for 30 more minutes. Stir in sugar, salt, and pepper. This dish is meant to be served with potato kneidel (recipe follows).

NUTRIENTS PER SERVING

195 calories, 1 gm. fat, 0 saturated fat, 0 cholesterol,
156 mg. sodium, 44 gm. carbohydrate, 2 gm. protein

Count as 1 fruit, 2 vegetable, and 1 bread/starch for
food exchange eating plans.

20 minutes "hands-on" preparation time, 50 minutes cooking time,
With potato kneidel (recipe follows), allow 55 minutes additional baking time

● ●

POTATO KNEIDEL
FAT-FREE!

(Meant to be prepared with Vegetarian Tzimmes)
Serves 12, 1 slice each

3 large russet potatoes

1 large egg, beaten or 1/4 cup
  liquid egg substitute

1/3 cup matzo meal

1/4 tsp. salt

1/4 tsp. pepper

Preheat oven to 325° F. Finely grate potatoes by hand. Put potatoes in a wire strainer or cheesecloth and squeeze out liquid. Combine grated potatoes, beaten egg, matzo meal, and salt and pepper in a large bowl. With moistened hands, form 2 large dumplings 3 to 4 inches in diameter. Mixture will not be dense enough to make into balls. Push vegetables to outer sides of the Dutch oven. Drop in the 2 large dumplings. Put Dutch oven, covered, in oven and cook until kneidel hold together well, about 45 minutes. Uncover, bake 10 more minutes, and serve. Each dumpling makes 6 slices.

NUTRIENTS PER SERVING

107 calories, 0 fat, 0 saturated fat, 17 mg. cholesterol with egg
(0 with egg sub.), 54 mg. sodium, 22 gm. carbohydrate, 2 gm. protein

Count as 1 1/2 bread/starch for food exchange eating plans.

20 minutes "hands-on" preparation time, 55 minutes baking time

CHOCOLATE-ALMOND MACAROONS

The original source of this recipe is Lori Tannenbaum,
former pastry chef at Michael's Restaurant in Santa Monica.
Serves 30, 1 cookie each

11 egg whites

3 cups sugar

2 Tbsp. apricot jam

2 tsp. vanilla extract

3/4 cup cocoa powder

3/4 cup powdered sugar

1 cup toasted sliced almonds

Preheat oven to 250° F. In large bowl of an electric mixer, beat egg whites until foamy. Gradually add sugar until mixture becomes very thick. When the sugar and egg-white mixture is very thick, add the apricot jam and vanilla. Sift together the cocoa and powdered sugar onto waxed paper. Add the cocoa mixture to the egg whites, and blend thoroughly. Fold in the toasted almonds. Dip an ice cream scoop in water and scoop batter onto brown-paper-lined baking sheets, 2 inches apart. Bake for 45 minutes or until the cookies are dry to the touch. Cool thoroughly before removing from the cookie sheets.

NUTRIENTS PER SERVING

162 calories, 4 gm. fat, 0 saturated fat, 0 cholesterol,
21 mg. sodium, 27 gm. carbohydrate, 3 gm. protein

Count as 2 fruit and 1 fat for food exchange eating plans.

20 minutes "hands-on" preparation time, 45 minutes baking time

Significant Symbols

CHRIST'S BIRTH

Our culture goes into overkill when celebrating Christ's simple manger birth. Instead of complaining about too many parties, too many cookies to bake, and too many presents to buy, welcome Christmas this year with a renewed focus on the reason for the season.

ADVENT WREATH

The traditional advent wreath supports five candles. One is lit on the fourth Sunday before Christmas. Each Sunday, another one is lit until Christmas Day when the Christ candle in the middle (and usually a contrasting color) is lit.

CHRISTMAS TREES

The custom of the Christmas tree began in Germany. Selecting a Christmas tree is most enjoyable when done leisurely with the whole family or a group of friends.

GIFTS FROM ST. NICK

St. Nicholas was a priest who lived in Asia Minor during the fourth century A.D. According to legend, he furnished dowries for three poor girls whose fathers couldn't afford to pay them. He did this at night by throwing sacks of coins into the girls' rooms. This is how the custom of nighttime visits from St. Nick originated. St. Nick's Day is celebrated on December 6 with simple gifts such as

Christmas stamps, music tapes, books, personalized ornaments, socks, napkins, and paper plates.

ADD FUN, SUBTRACT EXPENSE

◆ *Consider decorating your Christmas tree with paper chains, bread dough ornaments, cookies, popcorn strings, starched bows, decorated pine cones, or pretty Christmas cards.*

◆ *If you love to bake cookies, but shouldn't eat them, fasten cut out sugar cookies to a plain green wreath with some ribbon or fish line. Poke a tiny hole in the top of each cookie with a toothpick before you bake it. Decorate with colored sugar, bake, and cool.*

◆ *Prepare a video- or audiotaped greeting for special family members you won't see at Christmas. It will likely mean more than an expensive gift.*

◆ *Display Christmas books on open shelves. Open the Bible to Luke 2:1-20 and place a pretty bookmark at the place of the Christmas story.*

◆ *Collect one new Christmas CD or tape each year. Before long, you will have a collection that lasts the whole month. Enjoy singing traditional carols around the piano. Surely one family member will volunteer to pound out the right hand melody line.*

◆ *Spend some time at the Sunday dinner table or before bed reading Christmas cards together.*

MENU IDEAS

COME ANYTIME CHRISTMAS EVE CHEER

Cream of Crab Soup with Oyster Crackers

Cold Foods on a Bed of Red Cabbage Leaves:
Reduced-Fat Cheese, Reduced-Fat Summer Sausage,
Reduced-Fat Crackers

Italian Bean and Pesto Dip with Parmesan Canes

Not-Your-Grandma's Fruitcake

Bread Machine Chocolate Stollen

Flavored Cocoas

CHRISTMAS DAY DINNER

Roast Loin of Pork with Herbed Dried Cherry Glaze

Cran-Raspberry Sauce

Wild Rice Stuffing

Fluffy Dilled Carrots and Parsnips

Apple Rum Cheesecake

THE WEEKEND AFTER BRUNCH

Bread Machine Coffee Cake

Holiday Breakfast Burrito

Rudolph's Fruit Cups

THE WEEKEND AFTER LUNCH

Make it Easy Beef Hash or
Life-Saver Chicken

Red Cabbage Relish

CREAM OF CRAB SOUP

ONLY 2 GRAMS OF FAT

Serves 12, 1 cup each

2 Tbsp. margarine

1 small yellow onion, diced

2 stalks celery, diced

1 small green pepper, diced

1/4 cup minced fresh parsley

2 lb. diced crab meat or
  mock crab

1/2 cup flour

1 cup white wine

2 14-oz. cans evaporated
  skim milk

2 cups hot no-added-salt
  chicken broth

1/4 tsp. salt

1/2 tsp. white pepper

Melt margarine in a Dutch oven over medium heat. Sauté onion, celery, pepper, and parsley for 3 minutes. Add crab and flour, and blend well. Add wine and continue to stir until smooth. Add milk, chicken stock, salt, and pepper, and simmer for 10 minutes.

NUTRIENTS PER SERVING

*187 calories, 2 gm. fat, 0 saturated fat, 18 mg. cholesterol,
780 mg. sodium (remember that crabmeat is quite high in sodium),
25 gm. carbohydrate, 15 gm. protein*

*Count as 2 lean meat, 1 bread/starch, and 2 vegetable
for food exchange eating plans.*

15 minutes "hands-on" preparation time, 20 minutes cooking time

ITALIAN BEAN AND PESTO DIP WITH PARMESAN CANES

Serves 8

16-oz. can red kidney beans, drained and rinsed

1/2 cup cheddar-flavored cheese food

1/2 cup pesto

1 cup nonfat sour cream

1 small ripe, firm tomato, diced

1 green onion, diced

In a medium mixing bowl, coarsely mash beans with the back of a spoon or fork. Stir in the cheese, pesto, and 1/2 cup of sour cream. Spread the bean mixture on a large serving plate. Top with remaining sour cream, chopped tomato, and diced onions. Serve as a dip with Parmesan canes (recipe follows).

NUTRIENTS PER SERVING

144 calories, 4 gm. fat, 2 gm. saturated fat, 13 mg. cholesterol, 413 mg. sodium, 18 gm. carbohydrate, 9 gm. protein

Count as 1 bread/starch, 1 vegetable, and 1 fat for food exchange eating plans.

15 minutes "hands-on" preparation time

PARMESAN CANES

Serves 16, 1 cane each

11-oz. can refrigerated soft
  bread sticks
2 Tbsp. margarine, melted

1/2 cup grated Parmesan cheese
  (such as Kraft®)

Preheat oven to 350° F. Remove bread sticks from the tube, and cut into two 4-inch pieces. Dip pieces in melted margarine and then in grated cheese. Twist and shape into candy canes on an ungreased baking sheet. Bake for 16 minutes or until golden brown.

NUTRIENTS PER SERVING

105 calories, 5 gm. fat, 2 gm. saturated fat, 7 mg. cholesterol, 307 mg. sodium, 9 gm. carbohydrate, 4 gm. protein

Count as 1 bread/starch and 1/2 fat for food exchange eating plans.

10 minutes "hands-on" preparation time, 16 minutes baking time

NOT-YOUR-GRANDMA'S FRUITCAKE

This is described by originator Nancy Hill, R.D., as the ultimate holiday fruitcake for people who don't like candied fruit.

Serves 24

1 1/2 cups flour
1 cup sugar
1/2 tsp. salt
1 1/2 tsp. baking powder
3 cups pitted whole dates
1/3 cup large pecan halves

1 cup whole Brazil nuts
8-oz. jar whole maraschino
  cherries, drained
4 large ripe bananas
4 eggs or 1 cup liquid egg
  substitute

Preheat oven to 300° F. Sift flour with sugar, salt, and baking powder into a large bowl. Add dates, nuts, and maraschino cherries, and stir until the nuts and fruits are coated with the flour mixture. In another bowl, beat bananas until mashed. Add eggs to bananas, and continue beating until well blended and mixture is fluffy. Fold in flour mixture. Pour into a large loaf pan that has been sprayed with nonstick cooking spray. Pan will be very full. Bake for 1 3/4 to 2 hours or until cake springs back when center is touched. Cool in the pan on a rack for 15 minutes. Remove cake from pan. Cool completely, then wrap with foil, and store in a cool place. Allow cake to stand overnight before slicing.

NUTRIENTS PER SERVING

*278 calories, 9 gm. fat, 1 gm. saturated fat,
35 mg. cholesterol with egg (0 with egg sub.), 56 mg. sodium,
51 gm. carbohydrate, 5 gm. protein*

Count as 1 bread/starch, 2 fruit, and 1 1/2 fat for food exchange eating plans.

15 minutes "hands-on" preparation time, 2 hours baking time

BREAD MACHINE CHOCOLATE STOLLEN

Serves 24

DOUGH:

1/2 cup skim milk	1/3 cup sugar
1/4 cup water	3/4 tsp. salt
1 large egg	1 1/2 tsp. yeast
3 cups bread flour	1 Tbsp. vanilla
1/4 cup cocoa	2 Tbsp. soft margarine

• •

FILLING:

3/4 cup white chocolate morsels   2 Tbsp. all-fruit raspberry jam
1/4 cup chopped pecans

Measure ingredients for dough carefully, and dump into bread machine pan in order listed. Set machine for "Dough" program and push "Start." (Recipe tested with Hitachi Bread Machine.) Meanwhile, combine ingredients for filling, and set aside. When dough has been mixed, remove it from the bread machine pan. Roll it out on a floured surface to a 22- by 6-inch rectangle. With a sharp knife, cut it in half lengthwise to make two 22- by 3-inch strips. Spread half of the filling down the center length of each strip. Fold long sides of the dough over the filling, pinching seams and ends to seal. Place ropes, seam side down on a baking sheet that has been sprayed with nonstick cooking spray. Twist the ropes together, forming a round wreath, then pinch the ends to seal. Cover and let rise in a warm place for 45 minutes. Preheat oven to 350° F. Bake for 35 minutes. Allow stollen to rest at room temperature on the baking sheet for an additional 10 minutes before removing it to a wire rack to cool. For a double chocolate treat, serve this with Hershey's® flavored cocoas.

NUTRIENTS PER SERVING

138 calories, 4 gm. fat, 0 saturated fat, 9 mg. cholesterol, 85 mg. sodium, 21 gm. carbohydrate, 3 gm. protein

Count as 1 bread/starch and 1 fruit for food exchange eating plans.

15 minutes "hands-on" preparation time, 45 minutes rising time, 35 minutes baking time

••

ROAST LOIN OF PORK WITH HERBED DRIED CHERRY GLAZE

Serves 8, 3 oz. pork + 1/4 cup glaze each

2 to 2 1/2 lb. pork tenderloin roast

GLAZE:

1/2 cup dried cherries

1 1/2 cups applesauce

2 Tbsp. frozen cranberry juice cocktail concentrate

2 Tbsp. Dijon-style mustard

1/4 cup brown sugar

1 tsp. cinnamon

1/4 tsp. salt

1/4 tsp. ground cloves

Preheat oven to 325° F. Trim tenderloin well, and place on a rack above a roasting pan. Roast uncovered for 1 1/2 to 2 hours. In a small mixing bowl, combine ingredients for glaze, and set aside at room temperature while the meat roasts. This allows the cherries to become soft. Baste roast with glaze during final 30 minutes of roasting. Microcook remaining glaze in a glass or stoneware pouring vessel for 3 minutes on high power. Serve on the side with the sliced pork roast.

NUTRIENTS PER SERVING

266 calories, 5 gm. fat, 2 gm. saturated fat, 90 mg. cholesterol, 186 mg. sodium, 27 gm. carbohydrate, 28 gm. protein

Count as 3 lean meat and 1 1/2 fruit for food exchange eating plans.

10 minutes "hands-on" preparation time, 1 1/2 to 2 hours roasting time

CRAN-RASPBERRY SAUCE
FAT-FREE!

Serves 8, 1/3 cup each

1 lb. fresh cranberries	3/4 cup sugar
1 1/2 cups water	16-oz. pkg. frozen raspberries

In a 2-quart saucepan, combine cranberries and water, and bring to a boil. Boil for 5 minutes. Add sugar and raspberries, and boil for another 5 minutes. Pour into a heat-proof serving bowl, and chill at least 30 minutes. This sauce will be chunky. If you prefer a smooth sauce, process to the desired texture in a food processor before chilling.

NUTRIENTS PER SERVING

*156 calories, 0 fat, 0 saturated fat, 0 cholesterol,
1 mg. sodium, 38 gm. carbohydrate, 1 gm. protein*

Count as 2 1/2 fruit for food exchange eating plans

15 minutes "hands-on" preparation time, 30 minutes chilling time

WILD RICE STUFFING

Serves 8, 2/3 cup each

2 1/2 qt. water	1 large green pepper, chopped
3 cups uncooked wild rice	1 large red pepper, chopped
1 tsp. salt	2 stalks celery, chopped
1 Tbsp. vegetable oil	2 Tbsp. dried leaf sage, crumbled
1 large yellow onion, chopped	1/3 cup grated Parmesan cheese
4 cloves minced garlic or 1 tsp. dried minced garlic	

Preheat oven to 375° F. Boil water, add rice and salt; then cover and simmer for 15 minutes. Meanwhile, heat oil in a large non-stick skillet over medium heat. Sauté onions, garlic, peppers, and celery until soft. In a 3-quart casserole dish, combine cooked rice, vegetables, sage, and cheese. Bake for 40 minutes. Or microcook covered on high power for 15 minutes.

NUTRIENTS PER SERVING

209 calories, 5 gm. fat, 2 gm. saturated fat, 10 mg. cholesterol, 431 mg. sodium, 33 gm. carbohydrate, 10 gm. protein

Count as 2 bread/starch and 1 fat for food exchange eating plans.

20 minutes "hands-on" preparation time, 40 minutes baking time, 15 minutes microcooking time

FLUFFY DILLED CARROTS AND PARSNIPS

ONLY 2 GRAMS OF FAT

Fellow dietitian Lynda Vokaty contributed this.
Serves 8, 1/2 cup each

1 lb. carrots, peeled and sliced	1/2 tsp. salt
2 large parsnips, peeled and sliced	1/2 tsp. dried dillweed
1/4 cup skim milk	1/4 tsp. onion powder
1 Tbsp. soft margarine	1/8 tsp. white pepper

In a medium saucepan, bring 2 inches of water to boiling. Add carrots and parsnips. Return to boiling, then reduce heat to a simmer for 20 minutes. Drain vegetables. With an electric mixer on low speed, beat vegetables until smooth. Add milk and margarine during mixing. Stir in seasonings and serve.

NUTRIENTS PER SERVING

*108 calories, 2 gm. fat, 0 saturated fat, 0 cholesterol,
185 mg. sodium, 23 gm. carbohydrate, 2 gm. protein*

Count as 1 bread/starch and 1 vegetable for food exchange eating plans.

15 minutes "hands-on" preparation time, 20 minutes cooking time

APPLE RUM CHEESECAKE

Serves 16

1 1/2 cups crushed graham crackers

1 Tbsp. sugar

3 Tbsp. reduced-fat margarine, melted

8-oz. pkg. nonfat cream cheese, softened

1/2 cup sugar

2 eggs or 1/2 cup liquid egg substitute

1 tsp. vanilla

4 large MacIntosh apples, washed, peeled, and sliced thin

1 tsp. cinnamon

1/3 cup sugar

2 Tbsp. chopped pecans

1/3 cup apple jelly

2 tsp. rum extract

Preheat oven to 350° F. Combine graham cracker crumbs, sugar, and melted margarine. Press into the bottom of a 9-inch spring-form pan, and bake for 10 minutes. In a medium mixing bowl, combine softened cream cheese and sugar until well blended. Add the eggs and vanilla, blend well, and pour over baked crust. Toss apples with sugar and cinnamon. Spoon over cream cheese. Sprinkle with chopped nuts. Bake for 1 hour and 10 minutes. Remove from oven. Combine apple jelly and rum extract in a 1-cup glass measure. Microcook for 45 seconds to melt. Spoon over cheesecake. Refrigerate this dessert until serving time. Loosen cake from rim of pan and remove carefully.

NUTRIENTS PER SERVING

*180 calories, 7 gm. fat, 2 gm. saturated fat, 82 mg. cholesterol with egg
(5 mg. with egg sub.), 158 mg. sodium, 25 gm. carbohydrate, 5 gm. protein*

Count as 1 bread/starch, 1 fruit, and 1 fat for food exchange eating plans.

15 minutes "hands-on" preparation time, 1 hour and 20 minutes baking time

BREAD MACHINE COFFEE CAKE

ONLY 3 GRAMS OF FAT

Serves 24, 2 canes with 12 brunch-size pieces each

1 cup buttermilk	1/3 cup sugar
1 egg or 1/4 cup liquid egg substitute	1 1/2 tsp. dry yeast
	1/2 tsp. salt
3 cups flour	2 Tbsp. margarine

FILLING:

1/4 cup soft margarine	1 Tbsp. white sugar
1/2 cup brown sugar	2 tsp. cinnamon

GARNISH:

1/4 cup chopped red cherries, well drained	1/4 cup chopped green cherries, well drained

Remove bread machine pan from unit and add first seven ingredients in order given. Set machine for "Dough" or similar command. (This recipe was tested with a Hitachi bread machine.) Meanwhile, combine ingredients for the filling in a small bowl. When the machine has finished mixing the dough (approximately 1 1/2 hours), remove it from the pan and divide it into two equal parts. On a floured surface, roll each part into a 12- by 6-inch rectangle.

Place the dough on two baking sheets that have been sprayed with nonstick cooking spray. Make 2-inch cuts on the 12-inch sides of the dough at 1/2-inch intervals. Spread the filling down the center of each rectangle. Crisscross the strips over the filling, gently stretching each strip. Finally, curve the dough to form a candy cane shape, and sprinkle with chopped green and red cherries. Cover and allow dough to rise in a warm place for 30 minutes. Preheat oven to 375° F. Bake for 20 minutes.

NUTRIENTS PER SERVING

119 calories, 3 gm. fat, 1 gm. saturated fat, 10 mg. cholesterol with egg (1 mg. with egg sub.), 87 mg. sodium, 20 gm. carbohydrate, 3 gm. protein

Count as 1 bread/starch and 1 fat for food exchange eating plans.

30 minutes "hands-on" preparation time, 2 hours dough preparation and rising time, 20 minutes baking time

HOLIDAY BREAKFAST BURRITO

Serves 8

2 7-oz. cartons liquid egg
  substitute

1/2 cup chopped tomatoes (fresh
  or canned)

1 large onion, chopped

1/4 cup green pepper, chopped

1/3 cup chunky salsa

1/2 tsp. black pepper

8 8-inch flour tortillas

4 oz. reduced-fat cheddar cheese,
  shredded

Spray a large skillet with nonstick cooking spray. Pour in liquid egg substitute, tomatoes, onion, green pepper, and salsa. Cook over medium heat until firm. Season with black pepper. Stack the flour tortillas between very moist paper towels and microwave them on high for 2 minutes. Lay the heated tortillas out flat, spoon egg mixture on top, top with shredded cheese, and roll up. Place in an 11- by 7-inch glass baking dish that has been sprayed with nonstick cooking spray. Repeat for remaining tortillas. Microcook for 2 minutes on high power, and serve.

NUTRIENTS PER SERVING

*219 calories, 7 gm. fat, 2 gm. saturated fat, 11 mg. cholesterol,
472 mg. sodium, 25 gm. carbohydrate, 15 gm. protein*

*Count as 1 bread/starch, 2 lean meat, and 1 vegetable
for food exchange eating plans.*

*15 minutes "hands-on" preparation time,
2 minutes microcooking time*

RUDOLPH'S FRUIT CUPS

FAT-FREE!

Serves 8, 2/3 cup each

20-oz. can crushed pineapple

16-oz. pkg. frozen whole
strawberries

2 large ripe bananas, peeled
and sliced

12-oz. can sugar-free lemon lime
soft drink

4 whole maraschino cherries,
cut in half

In a large mixing bowl, combine crushed pineapple and juice, strawberries, sliced bananas, and soft drink. Ladle mixture into 8 freezer-safe plastic cups. Place 1 cherry in the middle of each cup. Freeze for at least 2 hours. Remove from freezer 1 hour before serving, or microcook 40 seconds each to a slush consistency for serving.

NUTRIENTS PER SERVING

*89 calories, 0 fat, 0 saturated fat, 0 cholesterol,
2 mg. sodium, 23 gm. carbohydrate, 1 gm. protein*

Count as 1 1/2 fruit for food exchange eating plans.

10 minutes "hands-on" preparation time, 2 hours freezing time

MAKE IT EASY BEEF HASH

Another delicious recipe from home economist Nancy Degner and my friends at the Beef Industry Council.

Serves 6, 1 cup each

1 lb. lean ground beef	1/2 tsp. salt
1 small onion, chopped	1/4 tsp. pepper
3 cups frozen potatoes O'Brien	1 cup prepared salsa

Brown ground beef and onion in a large skillet over medium heat for 10 minutes or until cooked through. Drain meat well. Stir in potatoes, salt, and pepper. Increase heat to medium-high, and cook 5 minutes, stirring occasionally. Stir in salsa and continue cooking 10 minutes until potatoes are lightly browned.

NUTRIENTS PER SERVING

244 calories, 10 gm. fat, 4 gm. saturated fat, 48 mg. cholesterol, 495 mg. sodium, 21 gm. carbohydrate, 16 gm. protein

Count as 1 bread/starch, 1 vegetable, 2 lean meat, and 1/2 fat for food exchange eating plans.

10 minutes "hands-on" preparation time, 25 minutes cooking time

LIFE-SAVER CHICKEN
ONLY 3 GRAMS OF FAT

Thank you, Teresa Nece.
Serves 8

8 skinless, boneless chicken
  breast halves
1 cup sweet and spicy reduced-
  calorie French dressing

1 cup canned cranberry sauce
1/2 pkg. dry onion soup mix

Preheat oven to 350° F. Place chicken breasts in a baking dish sprayed with nonstick cooking spray. In a small mixing bowl, combine dressing, cranberry sauce, and soup mix. Pour over the chicken breasts. Bake 45 minutes.

NUTRIENTS PER SERVING

221 calories, 3 gm. fat, 1 gm. saturated fat, 73 mg. cholesterol, 291 mg. sodium, 19 gm. carbohydrate, 27 gm. protein

Count as 3 lean meat and 1 fruit for food exchange eating plans.

15 minutes "hands-on" preparation time, 45 minutes baking time

RED CABBAGE RELISH

FAT-FREE!

Serves 16, 1/2 cup each

1 large navel orange, chopped fine

2 cups water

2 cups sugar

1 cup white vinegar

1-lb. bag cranberries

1 medium-size head red cabbage, cored and chopped medium-coarse

1 tsp. salt

1 cup dark raisins

1 tsp. ground coriander

1/8 tsp. ground cloves

Boil the orange and water in a large pan over medium heat until the orange is tender and most of the liquid is gone, about 20 minutes. Add sugar, vinegar, and cranberries to the pot. Bring to boiling. Add cabbage and salt. Return to boiling, and cook for 10 minutes. Add raisins, coriander, and cloves. Cook uncovered until cabbage is tender-crisp, about 10 minutes. Pack into 4 pint jars. Refrigerate the jars, and serve cold as a side dish. This keeps for 2 months.

NUTRIENTS PER SERVING

54 calories, 0 fat, 0 saturated fat, 0 cholesterol,
142 mg. sodium, 14 gm. carbohydrate, 1 gm. protein

Count as 1 fruit for food exchange eating plans.

15 minutes "hands-on" preparation time, 40 minutes cooking time

Significant Symbols

CLOCK STRIKES MIDNIGHT

At the stroke of midnight, the old year has ended. Hug your loved ones, or call someone special to wish them a happy new year. School-aged children love being part of the New Year's party and being allowed to stay up late.

ADD FUN, SUBTRACT EXPENSE

◆ *Instead of renting a motel room for a family party, invite your best friends and their air mattresses over for an old-fashioned slumber party!*

◆ *Review the year just passed by looking through photo albums and family videotapes together.*

MENU IDEAS

JUST SOUP FOR LUNCH

Cioppino or
Split Pea Soup or
French Onion Soup

FITS ANY PARTY!

Chicken Vegetable Burritos

Honey Mustard Wings

Hot Braunschweiger Spread

Chili Cheese Triangles

Sweet and Sour Meatballs

Cheesy Smoked Salmon Dip

Hot Artichoke Dip with French Bread Cubes

CIOPPINO

ONLY 2 GRAMS OF FAT

Serves 8, 1 cup each

1 Tbsp. vegetable oil

2 bunches green onions, diced fine

1 Tbsp. dried parsley

1/2 tsp. garlic powder

16-oz. can tomato sauce

1/2 cup dry white wine

1/4 tsp. salt

1/4 tsp. pepper

1 1/2 lb. white fish fillets, such as cod or orange roughy

In a large Dutch oven, sauté onions, parsley, and garlic in oil for 2 minutes. Add tomato sauce, wine, salt, and pepper, and simmer for 10 minutes. Wash fish fillets, then place in a single layer in the sauce, and simmer for 8 minutes, or until the fish flakes easily with a fork. Flake fish into bite-sized chunks, and serve.

NUTRIENTS PER SERVING

110 calories, 2 gm. fat, 0 saturated fat, 0 cholesterol, 545 mg. sodium, 7 gm. carbohydrate, 16 gm. protein

Count as 2 lean meat for food exchange eating plans.

10 minutes "hands-on" preparation time, 20 minutes cooking time

SPLIT PEA SOUP

Serves 12, 1 cup each

1 large yellow onion, diced	1/8 tsp. salt
2 stalks celery, chopped	1/4 tsp. pepper
1 Tbsp. dried parsley	2 qt. chicken broth
2 carrots, washed, peeled and diced	8 oz. very lean ham, diced
1 Tbsp. Worchestershire sauce	1 lb. split peas, washed and drained

Place all ingredients in a large Dutch oven and bring to a boil. Reduce heat to a simmer, and cook for 2 hours. Remove, cool and run through a food processor to desired consistency. Return mixture to the pot for reheating. Simmer for 10 minutes and serve.

NUTRIENTS PER SERVING

175 calories, 4 gm. fat, 1 gm. saturated fat, 11 mg. cholesterol, 1238 mg. sodium (to reduce sodium, omit salt and use reduced-sodium ham), 22 gm. carbohydrate, 13 gm. protein

Count as 1 bread/starch, 1 1/2 lean meat, and 1 vegetable for food exchange eating plans.

15 minutes "hands-on" preparation time, 2 hours and 10 minutes cooking time

FRENCH ONION SOUP
ONLY 3 GRAMS OF FAT

Serves 12, 1 cup each

8 strips bacon, diced fine	1/4 tsp. thyme
6 large yellow onions, sliced	1/4 tsp. salt
1/4 cup flour	1/4 tsp. pepper
1 1/2 qt. beef stock	1 cup white wine
2 cups water	2 cups plain bread croutons
4 bay leaves	1/2 cup grated Parmesan cheese

Cook bacon in a large Dutch oven until very crisp. Drain bacon well, set aside and remove most of the drippings from the pan. Sauté onions in the same pan until they begin to soften. Add flour, stirring constantly. Add stock and water until well-mixed. Add all seasonings, and let mixture cook approximately 1 hour. Add wine. Ladle hot soup into bowls and garnish with croutons, Parmesan cheese, and reserved bacon bits.

NUTRIENTS PER SERVING

115 calories, 3 gm. fat, 1 gm. saturated fat, 6 mg. cholesterol, 845 mg. sodium (to reduce sodium, omit salt), 15 gm. carbohydrate, 7 gm. protein

Count as 2 vegetable, 1/2 bread/starch, and 1/2 lean meat for food exchange eating plans.

15 minutes "hands-on" preparation time, 1 hour cooking time

CHICKEN VEGETABLE BURRITOS

Serves 8

8 fat-free flour tortillas

2 cups cooked, diced chicken breast meat

1-oz. pkg. taco seasoning mix

1/4 cup water

1/2 cup prepared salsa

10-oz. pkg. frozen corn, thawed

16-oz. can refried beans

4 oz. reduced-fat cheddar cheese, shredded

1 small head iceberg lettuce, shredded

1 large tomato, chopped

Preheat oven to 375° F. Remove tortillas from the refrigerator and set aside. In a large nonstick skillet, place chicken, taco seasoning, and water. Bring to a boil, then reduce heat and simmer uncovered for 5 minutes. Stir in salsa and corn. Spoon beans into tortillas, spreading smooth. Top with chicken mixture, and roll up, securing tortilla with a toothpick. Place tortillas in a baking dish that has been sprayed with nonstick cooking spray. Top with shredded cheese, and bake for 20 minutes. Serve hot with lettuce and tomato on the side.

NUTRIENTS PER SERVING

332 calories, 6 gm. fat, 3 gm. saturated fat, 56 mg. cholesterol, 893 mg. sodium, 42 gm. carbohydrate, 30 gm. protein

Count as 3 lean meat and 2 bread/starch for food exchange eating plans.

15 minutes "hands-on" preparation time, 20 minutes baking time

· ·

HONEY MUSTARD WINGS

Serves 8, 2 appetizers each

1 envelope dry onion soup mix   2 Tbsp. spicy brown mustard
1/3 cup honey   16 chicken wings

Preheat oven to 400° F. In a large bowl, combine soup mix, honey, and mustard. Set aside. Cut wings at joints and discard tips. Add wings to the soup mixture, and toss to coat. Place chicken in a baking pan that has been sprayed with nonstick cooking spray. Bake uncovered for 45 minutes, turning once.

NUTRIENTS PER SERVING

*186 calories, 9 gm. fat, 2 gm. saturated fat, 46 mg. cholesterol,
530 mg. sodium, 14 gm. carbohydrate, 14 gm. protein*

Count as 2 lean meat, 1 fruit, and 1/2 fat for food exchange eating plans.

15 minutes "hands-on" preparation time, 45 minutes baking time

HOT BRAUNSCHWEIGER SPREAD

ONLY 2 GRAMS OF FAT

Serves 24, 1 slice each

4 oz. braunschweiger sausage
4 oz. nonfat cream cheese
1/4 cup finely minced onion
1 tsp. sage

2 Tbsp. fresh minced parsley
24 slices cocktail rye bread
2 Tbsp. Dijon mustard

Preheat broiler on "High" setting. In a medium mixing bowl, beat first 5 ingredients until smooth. Spread mustard on rye bread, then spread with braunschweiger and cream cheese mixture. Place on a baking sheet and broil for 8 to 10 minutes, until lightly browned.

NUTRIENTS PER SERVING

43 calories, 2 gm. fat, 1 gm. saturated fat, 7 mg. cholesterol, 130 mg. sodium, 5 gm. carbohydrate, 2 gm. protein

Count as 1/2 bread/starch for food exchange eating plans.

15 minutes "hands-on" preparation time, 10 minutes broiling time

CHILI CHEESE TRIANGLES

Serves 15, 2 triangles each

10 flour tortillas, at room temperature

8 oz. nonfat cream cheese, softened to room temperature

15-oz. can chili with beans

6 oz. reduced-fat cheddar cheese, shredded

Preheat oven to 375° F. Spread tortillas with cream cheese, then sprinkle half of the tortilla with chili and shredded cheese. Gently fold tortilla in half to form a half moon shape. Press edges lightly with fingers to seal. Wrap in foil with all edges of foil sealed. Place foil-wrapped tortillas on a baking sheet, and bake for 10 to 15 minutes or until heated through. Cut into 3 wedges, and serve hot.

NUTRIENTS PER SERVING

154 calories, 6 gm. fat, 2 gm. saturated fat, 14 mg. cholesterol, 410 mg. sodium, 18 gm. carbohydrate, 9 gm. protein

Count as 1 1/2 lean meat and 1 bread/starch for food exchange eating plans.

15 minutes "hands-on" preparation time, 15 minutes baking time

SWEET AND SOUR MEATBALLS

Serves 24, 2 meatballs each

1 1/2 lb. lean ground beef

8-oz. can water chestnuts, drained and chopped

1 egg or 1/4 cup liquid egg substitute

1/3 cup dry bread crumbs

1 Tbsp. Worcestershire sauce

1 cup beer

1/2 cup brown sugar

1/4 cup vinegar

1/4 cup catsup

2 Tbsp. cornstarch

In a large bowl, combine ground beef, water chestnuts, eggs, bread crumbs, and Worcestershire sauce. Shape into 48 meatballs. Place on a broiling rack and broil for 6 minutes or until done. In a skillet, combine all remaining ingredients. Use a wire whisk to stir over medium heat, uncovered, until mixture thickens. Transfer broiled meatballs to a crockpot or chafing dish, then pour sauce over meatballs, and keep warm. Serve with toothpicks.

NUTRIENTS PER SERVING

101 calories, 4 gm. fat, 2 gm. saturated fat, 28 mg. cholesterol with egg (19 mg. with egg sub.), 92 mg. sodium, 9 gm. carbohydrate, 6 gm. protein

Count as 1 lean meat and 1 fruit for food exchange eating plans.

15 minutes "hands-on" preparation time, 6 minutes broiling time

CHEESY SMOKED SALMON DIP

Serves 8, 1/4 cup each

8-oz. pkg. reduced-fat cream
cheese, softened to room
temperature

8-oz. can smoked salmon,
drained and flaked

1 Tbsp. horseradish

4 drops hot sauce

1/4 cup catsup

Combine all ingredients in a mixing bowl. Transfer to a pretty serving bowl, and serve with melba rounds or reduced-fat party crackers.

NUTRIENTS PER SERVING

101 calories, 6 gm. fat, 3 gm. saturated fat, 17 mg. cholesterol, 468 mg. sodium, 4 gm. carbohydrate, 8 gm. protein

Count as 1 lean meat, 1 vegetable, and 1/2 fat for food exchange eating plans.

10 minutes "hands-on" preparation time

HOT ARTICHOKE DIP WITH FRENCH BREAD CUBES

8 servings, 1/2 cup dip + 1 slice bread each

1 Tbsp. vegetable oil

1 small onion, finely chopped

1/2 tsp. garlic powder

5 oz. canned artichoke hearts, well drained

4 small tomatoes, cored and chopped

3 Tbsp. minced fresh parsley

3 Tbsp. cider vinegar

2 oz. feta cheese, broken into pieces

1 medium loaf French bread, sliced into cubes

Heat oil in a skillet. Sauté onion, garlic powder, and artichoke hearts until onion is translucent. Add tomatoes, parsley, and vinegar. Heat through. Transfer dip to a crockpot or chafing dish. Garnish the top with feta cheese, and serve with cubes of French bread as dippers.

NUTRIENTS PER SERVING

130 calories, 4 gm. fat, 0 saturated fat, 6 mg. cholesterol, 246 mg. sodium, 19 gm. carbohydrate, 5 gm. protein

Count as 2 vegetable, 1 bread/starch, and 1/2 fat for food exchange eating plans.

15 minutes "hands-on" preparation time

Significant Symbols

PRESENTS

Choose one gift and put it at the person's place at the breakfast table to be opened as soon as the person's day begins. Give gifts of experience such as tickets to a concert or a gift certificate to a travel agency. Create a special poem for the celebrated person.

ADD FUN, SUBTRACT EXPENSE

◆ *Start the birthday or anniversary off with breakfast in bed and candles in the pancakes.*

◆ *Ask the birthday person to plan the menu for supper that night, or dine out at their favorite restaurant.*

◆ *Hide the gifts around the house.*

◆ *On each child's birthday, ask the child to describe special memories about the past year. Record the interview on cassette tape. On wedding anniversaries, record special memories of the marriage from that year.*

BIRTHDAY AND ANNIVERSARY RECIPES

BLT Dip

Veggie Spread for Crackers or Pita Bread

Bagel Rounds with Veggies and Cheese

Tex Mex Torta

Crab Puffs

Sour Cream Raspberry Salad

Spinach Salad with Sweet and Tangy Dressing

5 Low-fat Salad Dressings

Oven Barbecued Shrimp

Teriyaki Grilled Tuna with Mango

Fettucine Alfredo with Crab

Turkey Enchiladas

Chicken and Wild Rice Salad

Baked Rutabagas with Apple Cider

Kahlua Torte

BLT DIP

Serves 16, 1/4 cup each

8 strips bacon, diced	1 cup reduced-fat sour cream
1 cup reduced-fat mayonnaise	3 medium-size firm ripe tomatoes, peeled, seeded, and diced

In a medium skillet, cook diced bacon until crisp, then drain well. In a medium mixing bowl, combine cooked bacon with mayonnaise and sour cream. Gently fold in chunks of tomato. Transfer dip to a pretty serving bowl lined with lettuce leaves, and serve with melba rounds or reduced-fat party crackers.

NUTRIENTS PER SERVING

90 calories, 8 gm. fat, 3 gm. saturated fat, 8 mg. cholesterol, 167 mg. sodium, 3 gm. carbohydrate, 2 gm. protein

Count as 1 vegetable and 1 1/2 fat for food exchange eating plans.

15 minutes "hands-on" preparation time

VEGGIE SPREAD FOR CRACKERS OR PITA BREAD

Serves 8, 1/4 cup each

8-oz. pkg. reduced-fat
cream cheese

2 Tbsp. dill seed

1/2 tsp. white pepper

1 large stalk celery, finely
chopped

2 green onions, diced

1 large carrot, cleaned, peeled,
and shredded

1/2 small cucumber, peeled,
seeded, and diced

In a medium mixing bowl, combine cream cheese, dill seed, and pepper. Fold in vegetables, and refrigerate. Serve with crackers or toasted pita bread triangles.

NUTRIENTS PER SERVING

*70 calories, 5 gm. fat, 3 gm. saturated fat, 10 mg. cholesterol,
170 mg. sodium, 4 gm. carbohydrate, 3 gm. protein*

Count as 1 vegetable and 1 fat for food exchange eating plans.

15 minutes "hands-on" preparation time

BAGEL ROUNDS WITH VEGGIES AND CHEESE

Serves 16, 1/2 bagel each

8 bagels, sliced in half

8-oz. pkg. reduced-fat cream cheese

1/2 cup reduced-fat mayonnaise

2 tsp. dry buttermilk ranch salad dressing mix

2 cups finely chopped vegetables of choice (try broccoli, red onion, green pepper, and cauliflower)

Preheat oven to 400° F. Place bagel halves on a baking sheet, and bake for 10 to 15 minutes, until lightly toasted. Meanwhile in a small mixing bowl, combine cream cheese, mayonnaise, and salad dressing mix. Spread cream cheese mixture over bagel halves. Sprinkle with chopped vegetables, refrigerate, and serve.

NUTRIENTS PER SERVING

160 calories, 6 gm. fat, 2 gm. saturated fat, 5 mg. cholesterol, 327 mg. sodium, 22 gm. carbohydrate, 6 gm. protein

Count as 1 bread/starch, 1 vegetable, and 1 fat for food exchange eating plans.

15 minutes "hands-on" preparation time, 10 to 15 minutes baking time

TEX MEX TORTA

Serves 8, 1/2 tortilla each

4 large flour tortillas
2 tsp. chili powder
15-oz. can refried beans
4 oz. reduced-fat cheddar cheese
2 green onions, diced fine

3-oz. can green chiles, drained
1/2 cup reduced-fat sour cream
2 cups chopped lettuce

Preheat oven to 400° F. Lay tortillas on baking sheets. Spray generously with nonstick cooking spray. Sprinkle with chili powder, and bake for 8 to 10 minutes until golden. Cool. Divide next 6 ingredients into 4 parts, and layer on the toasted tortillas. Serve layered tortillas on a large plate and place it between 2 people sitting across from each other at a table. Both diners can break off pieces of the tortilla.

NUTRIENTS PER SERVING

176 calories, 6 gm. fat, 3 gm. saturated fat, 15 mg. cholesterol, 433 mg. sodium, 22 gm. carbohydrate, 11 gm. protein

Count as 1 bread/starch, 1 1/2 lean meat, and 1 vegetable for food exchange eating plans.

15 minutes "hands-on" preparation time, 10 minutes baking time

CRAB PUFFS

Serves 16, 1 puff each

8 English muffins, cut in half

1 cup garlic-flavored cheese
  spread

2 Tbsp. reduced-fat mayonnaise

8 oz. imitation crabmeat, diced

1 Tbsp. dill weed

Preheat broiler. Split English muffins in half and place on a baking sheet. Broil for 3 minutes or until golden brown. Measure cheese spread into a microwave-safe mixing bowl and microcook for 1 minute. Stir in mayonnaise and diced crabmeat. Spread crab mixture on top of broiled muffin halves. Sprinkle with dill weed. Broil another 4 minutes or until crab mixture begins to bubble. Serve hot.

NUTRIENTS PER SERVING

*127 calories, 4 gm. fat, 2 gm. saturated fat, 13 mg. cholesterol,
499 mg. sodium, 16 gm. carbohydrate, 6 gm. protein*

*Count as 1 lean meat and 1 bread/starch for
food exchange eating plans.*

10 minutes "hands-on" preparation time, 8 minutes broiling time

SOUR CREAM RASPBERRY SALAD

ONLY 2 GRAMS OF FAT

Serves 12

6-oz. pkg. raspberry gelatin or
  2 3-oz. pkg. sugar-free
  raspberry gelatin

1 cup hot water

16-oz. bag frozen whole raspberries

20-oz. can crushed pineapple,
  drained

1 pt. nonfat sour cream

2 tsp. almond extract

1/4 cup sugar

1/4 cup chopped pecans

Dissolve gelatin in the hot water in a large mixing bowl. Fold in berries and pineapple. Pour half of this mixture into an 11- by 7-inch glass dish. Refrigerate for 2 hours. Leave the remaining half of the gelatin mixture at room temperature. Mix sour cream with almond extract and sugar. Spread 1 1/2 cups of the sour cream mixture over the first layer of chilled gelatin, then cover with remaining gelatin. Refrigerate two more hours. Spread remaining 1/2 cup sour cream mixture on top. Garnish with chopped pecans. Cut in squares, and serve on a lettuce leaf.

NUTRIENTS PER SERVING USING SUGAR-FREE GELATIN

*100 calories, 2 gm. fat, 0 saturated fat, 0 cholesterol,
54 mg. sodium, 20 gm. carbohydrate, 3 gm. protein*

Count as 1/2 skim milk and 1 fruit for food exchange eating plans.

20 minutes "hands-on" preparation time, 4 hours chilling time

SPINACH SALAD WITH SWEET AND TANGY DRESSING

Serves 8, 1 cup each

10-oz. pkg. fresh spinach, torn into bite-sized pieces

2 large carrots, cleaned, peeled, and grated

DRESSING:

1/4 cup vegetable oil

1/3 cup red wine vinegar

2 tsp. lemon juice

2 tsp. soy sauce

1 tsp. sugar

1 tsp. dry mustard

1/2 tsp. curry powder

1/4 tsp. seasoned salt

1/2 tsp. pepper

2 cloves garlic, minced

Combine spinach with grated carrots in a large salad bowl. In a shaker container, mix ingredients for dressing. Pour dressing over spinach just before serving.

NUTRIENTS PER SERVING

77 calories, 7 gm. fat, 1 gm. saturated fat, 0 cholesterol, 185 mg. sodium, 5 gm. carbohydrate, 1 gm. protein

Count as 1 vegetable and 1 fat for food exchange eating plans.

15 minutes "hands-on" preparation time

HONEY GARLIC VINAIGRETTE DRESSING

ONLY 3 GRAMS OF FAT

All-purpose dressing for vegetable salads.
Yield: 2 cups (use 1/2 cup per 4-serving salad)

2 Tbsp. dried parsley (may substitute basil or another preferred herb)

1/4 cup olive oil

1 cup cider vinegar

2/3 cup honey

8 cloves garlic, minced

1/2 tsp. black pepper

Combine all ingredients in a shaker container, and mix well. Refrigerate after use.

NUTRIENTS PER SERVING

70 calories, 3 gm. fat, 0 saturated fat, 0 cholesterol, 1 mg. sodium, 12 gm. carbohydrate, 0 protein

Count as 1 fruit and 1/2 fat for food exchange eating plans.

10 minutes "hands-on" preparation time

PARMESAN GARLIC DRESSING

Add 2/3 cup Parmesan cheese to Honey Garlic Vinaigrette recipe

Combine all ingredients in a shaker container and mix well. Refrigerate after use.

NUTRIENTS PER SERVING

*84 calories, 4 gm. fat, 1 gm. saturated fat, 3 mg. cholesterol,
59 mg. sodium, 12 gm. carbohydrate, 1 gm. protein*

Count as 1 fruit and 1/2 fat for food exchange eating plans.

10 minutes "hands-on" preparation time

ITALIAN DRESSING
ONLY 3 GRAMS OF FAT

Add 1 tsp. oregano, 1 tsp. basil,
   and 1 tsp. fennel to Honey
   Garlic Vinaigrette recipe

Combine all ingredients in a shaker container, and mix well.
Refrigerate after use.

NUTRIENTS PER SERVING

*70 calories, 3 gm. fat, 0 saturated fat, 0 cholesterol,
1 mg. sodium, 12 gm. carbohydrate, 0 protein*

Count as 1 fruit and 1/2 fat for food exchange eating plans.

10 minutes "hands-on" preparation time

BUTTERMILK DRESSING

ONLY 1 GRAM OF FAT

Serves 8, 2 Tbsp. each

1/2 cup nonfat sour cream
1/4 cup buttermilk
1 Tbsp. reduced-fat mayonnaise

1 tsp. lemon juice
1/2 tsp. seasoned salt
1/2 tsp. black pepper

Whisk all ingredients together in a small mixing bowl. Transfer to a covered glass container.

NUTRIENTS PER SERVING

24 calories, 1 gm. fat, 0 saturated fat, 0 cholesterol, 175 mg. sodium, 4 gm. carbohydrate, 1 gm. protein

Count as 1/2 fruit for food exchange eating plans.

10 minutes "hands-on" preparation time

FRENCH DRESSING

FAT-FREE!

Serves 8, 1/4 cup each

1 can reduced-fat tomato soup
2 Tbsp. cider vinegar
1 tsp. basil
1/2 tsp. thyme
1 tsp. prepared mustard

1/4 tsp. garlic powder
1 tsp. Worcestershire sauce
1 tsp. lemon juice
1/4 tsp. black pepper

Combine all ingredients in a blender, processing until smooth. Refrigerate in a covered glass container.

NUTRIENTS PER SERVING

*10 calories, 0 fat, 0 saturated fat, 0 cholesterol,
44 mg. sodium, 2 gm. carbohydrate, 1 gm. protein*

Count as free for food exchange eating plans.

10 minutes "hands-on" preparation time

OVEN BARBECUED SHRIMP
ONLY 3 GRAMS OF FAT

Serves 8, 4 oz. shrimp each

2 lb. medium fresh or frozen
shrimp, thawed and peeled

1 Tbsp. soft margarine

2 Tbsp. catsup

1 Tbsp. Worcestershire sauce

1/2 tsp. finely grated lemon rind

1/4 tsp. garlic powder

2 tsp. dried parsley

1/2 tsp. paprika

1/4 tsp. oregano

1 bay leaf

1/4 tsp. cayenne pepper

Wash shrimp and spread out in a shallow baking dish. Combine all remaining ingredients in a saucepan, and bring to a boil. Reduce heat and simmer for 5 minutes. Remove bay leaf, then spoon sauce over the shrimp; cover and refrigerate for 30 minutes or up to overnight. When ready to bake, place shrimp and marinade in a 300° F. oven, and bake for 20 minutes or until shrimp is evenly translucent white. Do not overbake.

NUTRIENTS PER SERVING

*140 calories, 3 gm. fat, 1 gm. saturated fat, 174 mg. cholesterol,
320 mg. sodium, 2 gm. carbohydrate, 23 gm. protein*

Count as 3 lean meat for food exchange eating plans.

*15 minutes "hands-on" preparation time, 30 minutes marinating time,
20 minutes baking time*

TERIYAKI GRILLED TUNA WITH MANGO

Serves 8

8 4-oz. tuna steaks, cut
1-inch thick

1 fresh mango, peeled and cut
into thin slices

1 green pepper, cut into thin slices

MARINADE:

1/4 cup sugar

1/4 cup reduced-sodium soy sauce

1/4 cup dry sherry

1/2 tsp. ground ginger

Place tuna steaks in a shallow pan. Combine ingredients for the marinade in a small saucepan. Bring to a boil and boil for 5 minutes. Pour 1/2 cup of marinade over tuna, then cover and refrigerate for at least 30 minutes or up to overnight. Refrigerate extra marinade until ready to grill. When ready to grill, grill tuna steaks 5 inches from medium flame, 6 minutes on each side. During last 2 minutes of grilling, top each steak with slivers of mango and pepper, and drizzle with reserved marinade.

NUTRIENTS PER SERVING

*218 calories, 6 gm. fat, 2 gm. saturated fat, 43 mg. cholesterol,
343 mg. sodium, 12 gm. carbohydrate, 28 gm. protein*

Count as 4 lean meat for food exchange eating plans.

*15 minutes "hands-on" preparation time,
30 minutes marinating time, 12 minutes grilling time*

FETTUCINE ALFREDO WITH CRAB

Serves 8, 1/4 cup each

1 1/2 cups 1% cottage cheese

1 cup evaporated skimmed milk

1/2 tsp. garlic powder

3 Tbsp. flour

1 Tbsp. lemon juice

1 1/2 tsp. dried basil

1/2 tsp. dry mustard

1/2 tsp. white pepper

1/2 tsp. salt

2 lb. diced, cooked crabmeat

12 oz. fettucine

GARNISH: 2 ripe medium size tomatoes, peeled, seeded, and chopped

In a blender container, puree cottage cheese with evaporated skim milk. Add garlic, flour, lemon juice, basil, mustard, pepper, and salt. Process until well blended. Pour into a medium stockpot, and cook over medium heat until thickened. Be careful not to boil. Fold in diced crab, and heat through. Meanwhile, prepare fettucine according to package directions, being careful not to overcook. Drain noodles, and spoon onto plates. Spoon sauce over noodles, and garnish with chopped tomatoes.

NUTRIENTS PER SERVING

328 calories, 4 gm. fat, 1 gm. saturated fat, 116 mg. cholesterol, 740 mg. sodium, 37 gm. carbohydrate, 36 gm. protein

Count as 3 lean meat, 1 bread/starch, and 1 vegetable for food exchange eating plans.

20 minutes "hands-on" preparation time

TURKEY ENCHILADAS

Serves 8

10-oz. can reduced-fat cream of chicken soup

1/2 cup nonfat sour cream

1 Tbsp. flour

4 green onions, diced fine

2 cups diced cooked turkey

16-oz. pkg. frozen mixed vegetables, thawed

8 large flour tortillas

4 oz. reduced-fat American cheese, shredded

Preheat oven to 350° F. Spray a 9- by 13-inch pan with nonstick cooking spray. In a medium saucepan, combine chicken soup, sour cream, flour, and green onions. Cook over medium heat until mixture is bubbly, stirring constantly. Stir in turkey and mixed vegetables. Spoon filling into 8 tortillas and roll up. Place seam side down in the prepared pan. Sprinkle with cheese. Cover and bake for 30 minutes. Uncover for 5 minutes to brown cheese.

NUTRIENTS PER SERVING

319 calories, 7 gm. fat, 2 gm. saturated fat, 45 mg. cholesterol, 757 mg. sodium, 37 gm. carbohydrate, 27 gm. protein

Count as 2 1/2 lean meat, 2 bread/starch, and 1 vegetable or food exchange eating plans.

15 minutes "hands-on" preparation time, 35 minutes baking time

CHICKEN AND WILD RICE SALAD

Serves 8, 1 cup each

1 cup uncooked wild rice

1/2 tsp. seasoned salt

2 cups cooked diced chicken

1 1/2 cups green grapes, cut in half

8-oz. can sliced water chestnuts, drained well

8-oz. can pineapple tidbits, drained well

1/2 tsp. curry powder

2/3 cup reduced-fat mayonnaise

Cook rice with seasoned salt in boiling water until tender, about 40 minutes. Drain and rinse with cold water. Drain again. In a large salad bowl, combine cooked rice with chicken, grapes, water chestnuts, and pineapple. In a small bowl, stir curry powder into mayonnaise. Fold mayonnaise into rice and chicken mixture. Serve on red lettuce or red cabbage leaves.

NUTRIENTS PER SERVING

246 calories, 9 gm. fat, 2 gm. saturated fat, 48 mg. cholesterol, 317 mg. sodium, 22 gm. carbohydrate, 20 gm. protein

Count as 2 lean meat, 1 fruit, and 1 bread/starch for food exchange eating plans.

15 minutes "hands-on" preparation time, 30 minutes cooking time

BAKED RUTABAGAS WITH APPLE CIDER

ONLY 2 GRAMS OF FAT

Serves 8, 1/2 cup each

1 Tbsp. soft margarine

1 large onion, sliced thin

2 lb. rutabagas, peeled, quartered, and thinly sliced

1/2 cup apple cider

2 Tbsp. cider vinegar

1/4 cup apple jelly

Preheat oven to 350° F. Heat margarine in a large skillet over medium heat. Add onions and sauté until soft. Meanwhile, bring a large pot of water to a boil. Add sliced rutabagas and cook for 8 minutes. Drain well. Add all remaining ingredients to the skillet, and simmer over medium-high heat for 8 minutes. Spray a 2-quart casserole dish with nonstick cooking spray. Transfer cooked rutabagas to the dish and pour apple cider sauce over top. Bake for 20 minutes or until bubbly.

NUTRIENTS PER SERVING

90 calories, 2 gm. fat, 0 saturated fat, 0 cholesterol, 31 mg. sodium, 18 gm. carbohydrate, 2 gm. protein

Count as 1 fruit and 1 vegetable for food exchange eating plans.

15 minutes "hands-on" preparation time, 20 minutes cooking time, 20 minutes baking time

KAHLUA TORTE

Serves 16

18-oz. pkg. reduced-fat white cake mix, prepared according to package directions in 2 8-inch round pans

5 Tbsp. kahlua

1/2 cup semi-sweet chocolate chips

1/4 cup powdered sugar

GARNISH: 1/4 cup flaked coconut

In a small pan, heat kahlua over medium heat until bubbles form around the edge. Do not boil. In a blender container, combine Kahlua with the chocolate chips. Process until the mixture is smooth. Add powdered sugar and blend again. Transfer the mixture to a small bowl. Cover and refrigerate for about an hour or until it reaches a spreadable consistency. Place one layer of cake on a serving plate. Spread half of chocolate on cake. Place second cake on top. Spread remaining chocolate on top. Garnish with coconut, slice and serve.

NUTRIENTS PER SERVING

186 calories, 4 gm. fat, 0 saturated fat, 0 cholesterol, 236 mg. sodium, 32 gm. carbohydrate, 3 gm. protein

Count as 1 bread/starch, 1 fruit, and 1 fat for food exchange eating plans.

20 minutes "hands-on" preparation time, 1 hour chilling time, 30 minutes baking time

HOLIDAYS ARE FOR KIDS TOO!

MENU IDEAS

Real Lemonade

Raspberry Froth

Low-Fat Chex® Mix

Creamy Fruit Dip

Microwave Caramel Corn

Sticky Buns

Cabbage Apple Salad

Joan's Apple Toss Salad

Orange Sherbet Salad

Green Beans in Mushroom Soup

Cheesy Mashed Potatoes

Make Your Own Pizza

Nonfat Brownies

Microwave Baked Apples

Low-Fat Rice Krispie® Bars

REAL LEMONADE

FAT-FREE!

Serves 8, 1 cup each

1 tsp. grated lemon rind
4 fresh lemons, squeezed for juice
3/4 cup sugar

5 cups water
1 cup ice cubes
GARNISH: thin lemon slices

Combine lemon rind, juice from lemons, and sugar in a quart-size glass measure. Stir to dissolve sugar. Refrigerate, covered, until ready to serve. Pour chilled syrup into a quart pitcher, add water and ice cubes, and serve. Garnish glasses with lemon slices.

NUTRIENTS PER SERVING

71 calories, 0 fat, 0 saturated fat, 0 cholesterol, 0 sodium, 20 gm. carbohydrate, 0 protein

Count as 1 fruit for food exchange eating plans.

10 minutes "hands-on" preparation time

RASPBERRY FROTH

ONLY 1 GRAM OF FAT

Serves 8, 1 cup each

1 qt. raspberry sherbet

2 qt. sugar-free lemon-lime soft drink

Spoon 1/2 cup of sherbet into each of eight 10-oz. party cups. Pour sugar-free lemon-lime soft drink over the sherbet. Put in a straw and a spoon, and serve.

NUTRIENTS PER SERVING

130 calories, 1 gm. fat, 0 saturated fat, 0 cholesterol, 30 mg. sodium, 28 gm. carbohydrate, 1 gm. protein

Count as 2 fruit for food exchange eating plans.

10 minutes "hands-on" preparation time

LOW-FAT CHEX® MIX

Serves 8, 1/2 cup each

2 cups Rice Chex® cereal

2 cups Corn Chex® cereal

2 cups Wheat Chex® cereal

2 cups mini-knot pretzels

3 Tbsp. reduced-fat margarine, melted

1/4 tsp. garlic powder

1/4 tsp. seasoned salt

2 tsp. lemon juice

4 tsp. Worcestershire sauce

Preheat oven to 325° F. Combine cereals with pretzels in a 13- by 9-inch metal pan. Combine remaining ingredients in a small bowl, and pour over the cereal mixture. Stir gently until well coated. Bake for 45 minutes, stirring every 15 minutes. Spread on paper towels to cool. Store in a covered plastic container.

NUTRIENTS PER SERVING

147 calories, 4 gm. fat, 0 saturated fat, 0 cholesterol, 530 mg. sodium, 24 gm. carbohydrate, 3 gm. protein

Count as 2 bread/starch for food exchange eating plans.

10 minutes "hands-on" preparation time, 45 minutes baking time

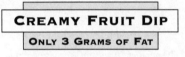

CREAMY FRUIT DIP

ONLY 3 GRAMS OF FAT

Serves 8, 1/4 cup each

2 large pears, cored
1/4 cup plain low-fat yogurt
4 oz. reduced-fat cream cheese

1 tsp. finely grated lemon peel
1/4 cup powdered sugar

Combine all ingredients in a blender container, and process until smooth. Pour into a serving dish, and serve with apple wedges, pineapple chunks, and melon balls.

NUTRIENTS PER SERVING

74 calories, 3 gm. fat, 2 gm. saturated fat, 6 mg. cholesterol, 85 mg. sodium, 12 gm. carbohydrate, 2 gm. protein

Count as 1 fruit for food exchange eating plans.

15 minutes "hands-on" preparation time

MICROWAVE CARAMEL CORN

Serves 10, 2 cups each

20 cups popped corn

1 cup packed brown sugar

1/4 cup light corn syrup

1/2 tsp. salt

1/2 cup reduced-fat margarine

1 tsp. vanilla

1/2 tsp. baking soda

Spray the inside of a large brown paper bag with nonstick cooking spray. Add popped corn. Combine sugar, syrup, salt, and margarine in a quart-size glass measuring cup. Microcook on high for 2 minutes. Stir, and microwave again for 3 more minutes. Add vanilla and baking soda. Stir well. Pour sugar mixture over the popcorn, and stir with a long-handled wooden spoon. Fold the top of the sack. Place in microwave oven and microcook on high power for 1 minute. Shake, then cook again for 1 minute. Shake, and cook for 30 seconds, shake again, and cook for 30 more seconds. Pour onto aluminum foil and let cool.

NUTRIENTS PER SERVING

*204 calories, 5 gm. fat, 1 gm. saturated fat, 0 cholesterol,
263 mg. sodium, 40 gm. carbohydrate, 2 gm. protein*

Count as 2 bread/starch and 1 fat for food exchange eating plans.

20 minutes "hands-on" preparation time

STICKY BUNS

ONLY 3 GRAMS OF FAT

Serves 12

1 lb. frozen white bread dough

2 Tbsp. reduced-fat margarine

1/4 cup brown sugar

3 Tbsp. corn syrup

1 tsp. cinnamon

1/2 cup raisins

1/4 cup sugar mixed with
   1/2 tsp. cinnamon

Defrost bread dough according to package directions. Place margarine in a 9-inch metal cake pan. Place over low heat until melted. Remove from heat and stir in brown sugar, 2 tablespoons of corn syrup, and cinnamon. Roll dough out on a floured surface into a 12- by 9-inch rectangle. Drizzle remaining corn syrup over the dough. Sprinkle with raisins, and the sugar and cinnamon mixture. Roll dough up, jelly-roll fashion, starting with the longest side. Cut crosswise into 12 pieces. Arrange, cut side down in the prepared pan. Let rise in a warm place for 1 hour or in the refrigerator overnight. Preheat oven to 350° F. Bake for 25 minutes or until golden brown.

NUTRIENTS PER SERVING

*191 calories, 3 gm. fat, 0 saturated fat, 0 cholesterol,
306 mg. sodium, 37 gm. carbohydrate, 4 gm. protein*

Count as 1/2 fruit and 2 bread/starch for food exchange eating plans.

*20 minutes "hands-on" preparation time, 1 hour rising time,
25 minutes baking time*

CABBAGE APPLE SALAD

ONLY 3 GRAMS OF FAT

*Debra Ohrt added colored marshmallows to
cabbage salad to win kid approval.*
Serves 12, 3/4 cup each

1 lb. shredded cabbage

1 red Delicious apple, cored and
cut into chunks

1 cup green grapes, halved

1 cup colored mini-marshmallows

1/2 cup reduced-fat mayonnaise

2 Tbsp. skim milk

2 Tbsp. sugar

Combine first four ingredients in a large salad bowl. In a small
mixing bowl, combine mayonnaise with skim milk and sugar. Pour
over cabbage, and stir to coat. Serve or refrigerate for up to 1 hour
before serving.

NUTRIENTS PER SERVING

*127 calories, 3 gm. fat, 1 gm. saturated fat, 0 cholesterol,
84 mg. sodium, 25 gm. carbohydrate, 1 gm. protein*

*Count as 1 fruit, 2 vegetable, and 1/2 fat for
food exchange eating plans.*

10 minutes "hands-on" preparation time

JOAN'S APPLE TOSS SALAD
ONLY 2 GRAMS OF FAT

For Stephen, Kathleen, Molly, and Patrick Shannon.
Serves 8, 1/2 cup each

2 large Golden Delicious apples,
washed, peeled and chopped

2 Tbsp. chopped peanuts

1 large stalk celery, diced

1 large carrot, washed, peeled, and
shredded

1/2 cup raisins

1 cup fat-free lemon-flavored
yogurt

Combine all ingredients in a salad bowl and mix to coat. Serve, or
refrigerate up to 1 hour before serving.

NUTRIENTS PER SERVING

91 calories, 2 gm. fat, 0 saturated fat, 1 mg. cholesterol,
31 mg. sodium, 17 gm. carbohydrate, 3 gm. protein

Count as 1 1/2 fruit for food exchange eating plans.

15 minutes "hands-on" preparation time

ORANGE SHERBET SALAD

ONLY 1 GRAM OF FAT

This recipe was a gift from Marsha.
Serves 8, 1/2 cup each

2 3-oz. pkgs. sugar-free
  orange gelatin
2 cups boiling water

2 cups orange sherbet
11-oz. can mandarin oranges,
  drained well

In a large mixing bowl, combine gelatin with boiling water. Stir until gelatin is completely dissolved. Add sherbet, and stir until it melts. Add drained mandarin oranges, and pour into a glass serving bowl. Chill for at least 2 hours or until the mixture is set.

NUTRIENTS PER SERVING

91 calories, 1 gm. fat, 1 gm. saturated fat, 3 mg. cholesterol, 26 mg. sodium, 21 gm. carbohydrate, 1 gm. protein

Count as 1 1/2 fruit for food exchange eating plans.

15 minutes "hands-on" preparation time, 2 hours chilling time

GREEN BEANS IN MUSHROOM SOUP

Serves 8, 1/2 cup each

2 16-oz. cans French-cut green
  beans, well drained
13-oz. can reduced-fat cream of
  mushroom soup

1/2 cup skim milk
1 tsp. Worcestershire sauce
1/2 cup French-fried onion rings

Preheat oven to 350° F. Empty drained beans into an 11- by 7-inch baking dish. In a small mixing bowl, combine soup, milk, and

Worcestershire sauce. Pour soup mixture over the beans, folding gently to coat beans. Sprinkle with onion rings. Bake for 25 minutes. To microcook: microwave on 70% power for 12-15 minutes or until mixture is bubbly.

NUTRIENTS PER SERVING

85 calories, 4 gm. fat, 1 gm. saturated fat, 1 mg. cholesterol, 533 mg. sodium, 10 gm. carbohydrate, 2 gm. protein

Count as 2 vegetable and 1 fat for food exchange eating plans.

10 minutes "hands-on" preparation time, 25 minutes baking time or 15 minutes microcooking time

CHEESY MASHED POTATOES

Serves 8, 1/2 cup each

3 large potatoes, washed, peeled, quartered and cooked

3 Tbsp. skim milk

1 Tbsp. reduced-fat margarine

4 oz. processed cheese spread

Preheat oven to 350° F. Combine tender-cooked potatoes with milk and margarine, and beat with an electric mixer until fluffy. Sir in cheese spread. Spoon into a 2-quart casserole. Bake for 20 minutes or until heated through.

NUTRIENTS PER SERVING

92 calories, 4 gm. fat, 2 gm. saturated fat, 8 mg. cholesterol, 253 mg. sodium, 11 gm. carbohydrate, 3 gm. protein

Count as 1 bread/starch for food exchange eating plans.

10 minutes "hands-on" preparation time, 20 minutes baking time

MAKE YOUR OWN PIZZA

A recipe perfected by my dear neighbor,
Deb Moser, for her crew and mine.
Serves 12, makes 2 pizzas

4 pkg. Robin Hood® pizza crust mix, prepared according to package directions

24 oz. your favorite pizza or spaghetti sauce

PIZZA TOPPINGS OF YOUR CHOICE:

1 lb. ground beef, browned and drained, or

1 lb. thin-sliced pepperoni or

1 lb. lean Canadian bacon

Diced green peppers

Diced onions

Canned mushroom pieces, drained

1 lb. shredded part-skim mozzarella cheese

Preheat oven to 400° F. Prepare crusts according to package directions. Divide mixture between two 12-inch pizza pans that have been sprayed with nonstick cooking spray. Bake for 15 minutes and remove from the oven. Spread with pizza sauce, then let the kids sprinkle on their desired toppings and shredded cheese. Bake for 20 to 25 more minutes.

NUTRIENTS PER SERVING
(NUTRIENT ANALYSIS COMPLETED WITH REDUCED-FAT RAGU® SAUCE AND LEAN GROUND BEEF AS TOPPING)

321 calories, 12 gm. fat, 6 gm. saturated fat, 48 mg. cholesterol, 329 mg. sodium, 29 gm. carbohydrate, 23 gm. protein

Count as 1 1/2 bread/starch, 1 vegetable, and 3 lean meat for food exchange eating plans.

15 minutes "hands-on" preparation time, 40 minutes baking time

NONFAT BROWNIES

FAT-FREE!

*This recipe was donated to the Iowa Dietetic Association cookbook by
Cindy McClary, R.D., from Sioux City, Iowa.*

Serves 12

1/2 cup unsweetened applesauce
1 cup sugar
2 egg whites
1/2 tsp. vanilla
3/4 cup flour

1/4 cup cocoa
1/4 tsp. baking powder
1/8 tsp. salt
GARNISH: powdered sugar

Spray a 9-inch square baking pan with nonstick cooking spray. Set aside. In a large mixing bowl, combine applesauce, sugar, egg whites, and vanilla. Stir in flour, cocoa, baking powder, and salt. Pour into prepared pan, and bake for 20 minutes. Sprinkle with powdered sugar when cool.

NUTRIENTS PER SERVING

*104 calories, 0 fat, 0 saturated fat, 0 cholesterol,
43 mg. sodium, 25 gm. carbohydrate, 2 gm. protein*

Count as 1 bread/starch and 1/2 fruit for food exchange eating plans.

10 minutes "hands-on" preparation time, 20 minutes baking time

MICROWAVE BAKED APPLES

ONLY 3 GRAMS OF FAT

Serves 8, 1/2 cup each

3 large baking apples, cored
and quartered

1/4 cup reduced-fat margarine

1/2 cup oatmeal

1/4 cup brown sugar

Place quartered apples in a 9-inch square microwave-safe baking dish that has been sprayed with nonstick cooking spray. In a small bowl, mix margarine, oatmeal, and brown sugar together until crumbly. Pour oatmeal mixture over the apples, cover, and microcook on high power for 8 to 10 minutes. Serve hot with low-fat vanilla frozen yogurt.

NUTRIENTS PER SERVING

*99 calories, 3 gm. fat, 1 gm. saturated fat, 0 cholesterol,
55 mg. sodium, 18 gm. carbohydrate, 1 gm. protein*

Count as 1 fruit and 1/2 fat for food exchange eating plans.

10 minutes "hands-on" preparation time, 10 minutes microcooking time

LOW-FAT RICE KRISPIE® BARS
ONLY 1 GRAM OF FAT

Serves 16

2 Tbsp. reduced-fat margarine   2 Tbsp. corn syrup
40 large marshmallows   6 cups Rice Krispies® cereal

Spray a 13- by 9-inch baking pan with nonstick cooking spray. Put margarine in a large mixing bowl and microcook for 20 seconds. Add marshmallows and corn syrup, and mix well. Microcook on high power for 1 1/2 minutes or until mixture is smooth when stirred. Immediately add cereal, mixing lightly until well-coated. Spread mixture into the baking pan, let stand for 30 minutes, then cut into squares.

NUTRIENTS PER SERVING

*113 calories, 1 gm. fat, 0 saturated fat, 0 cholesterol,
101 mg. sodium, 26 gm. carbohydrate, 1 gm. protein*

Count as 1 bread/starch and 1/2 fruit for food exchange eating plans.

*10 minutes "hands-on" preparation time,
2 minutes microcooking time*

BIBLIOGRAPHY

Becker, Joyce. *Jewish Holiday Crafts*. New York: Bonim Books, 1977.

Bennett, Steve and Ruth. *365 TV-Free Activities*. Holbrook, MA: Bob Adams, Inc. Publishers, 1991.

Chambers, Wicke. *The Celebration Book of Great American Traditions*. New York: Harper and Row, 1983.

Davidoff, Henry. *Pocket Book of Quotations*. New York: Pocket Books, 1952.

Diller, Harriett. *Celebrations That Matter*. Minneapolis: Augsburg, 1990.

Gaither, Gloria and Dobson, Shirley. *Let's Make a Memory*. Dallas: Word Publishing, 1983.

King, Coretta Scott. *My Life with Martin Luther King, Jr.* New York: Holt, 1969.

Klapthor, Margaret. *The First Ladies' Cookbook*. New York: Parent's Magazine Press, 1975.

Krythe, Maymie. *All About American Holidays*. New York: Harper and Row, 1962.

McWilliams, John-Roger and Peter. *Do It!* Los Angeles: Prelude Press, 1991.

Ojakanagas, Beatrice. *Great Holiday Baking Book*. New York: Clarkson Potter/Publishers, 1994.

Syme, Ronald. *Columbus*. New York: William Morrow and Company, 1952.